GENERAL
CONFERENCE
ADDRESSES

———

GENERAL CONFERENCE ADDRESSES

JOURNAL EDITION
OCTOBER 2021

DESERET
BOOK

SALT LAKE CITY, UTAH

CONTENTS

SATURDAY EVENING SESSION

SUNDAY MORNING SESSION

SUNDAY AFTERNOON SESSION

SATURDAY MORNING SESSION

OCTOBER 2, 2021

PURE TRUTH, PURE DOCTRINE, AND PURE REVELATION

PRESIDENT RUSSELL M. NELSON

President of The Church of Jesus Christ of Latter-day Saints

My dear brothers and sisters, welcome to general conference! What a joy it is to be with you! You have been on my mind almost constantly during the past six months. I have prayed *about* you and *for* you. During recent weeks I have prayed intently that this conference would be a time of revelation and reflection for all who seek those blessings.

We are delighted to be speaking to you from the Conference Center once again. Most of the seats remain empty, but the presence of some members of the Tabernacle Choir is a wonderful step forward. We welcome you all to this largely virtual conference, wherever you are.

We are still dealing with the ravages of COVID-19 and its variants. We thank you for following our counsel and the advice of medical experts and government officials in your own communities.

We convene each general conference as directed by the Lord.[1] The format has varied over the years. When I was much younger, conference lasted three or four days. Later, conference was reduced to two days. Every message—then and now—is the result of earnest prayer and much spiritual preparation.

The General Authorities and General Officers of the Church who speak will focus their messages on our Savior, Jesus Christ, His mercy, and His infinite redeeming power. There has never been a time in the history of the world when knowledge of our Savior is more personally vital and relevant to *every human soul*. Imagine how quickly the devastating conflicts throughout the world—and those in our individual lives—would be resolved if we all chose to follow Jesus Christ and heed His teachings.

In that spirit, I invite you to listen for three things during this conference: pure truth, the pure doctrine of Christ, and pure revelation. Contrary to the doubts of some, there really *is* such a thing as right and wrong. There really *is* absolute truth—eternal truth. One of the plagues of our day is that too few people know where to turn for truth.[2] I can assure you that what you will hear today and tomorrow constitutes pure truth.

The pure doctrine of Christ is powerful. It changes the life of everyone who understands it and seeks to implement it in his or her life. The doctrine of Christ helps us find and stay on the covenant path. Staying on that narrow but well-defined path will ultimately qualify us to receive all that God has.[3] Nothing could be worth more than *all* our Father has!

Finally, pure revelation for the questions in your heart will make this conference rewarding and unforgettable. If you have not yet sought for the ministering of the Holy Ghost to help you hear what the Lord would have you hear during these two days, I invite you to do so now. Please make this conference a time of feasting on messages from the Lord through His servants. Learn how to apply them in your life.

This *is* The Church of Jesus Christ of Latter-day Saints. We are His covenant people. The Lord declared that He would hasten His work in its time,[4] and He is doing so at an ever-increasing pace. We are privileged to participate in His holy work.

I invoke a blessing upon all who are seeking greater light, knowledge, and truth. I express my love for each of you, in the sacred name of Jesus Christ, amen.

Notes

1. See Doctrine and Covenants 20:61, 64, 67; 26:1.
2. See Doctrine and Covenants 123:12.
3. See Ether 4:14; Doctrine and Covenants 78:17–18; 84:38.
4. See Doctrine and Covenants 88:73.

THE GREATEST POSSESSION

ELDER JEFFREY R. HOLLAND
Of the Quorum of the Twelve Apostles

The scriptures speak of a rich young ruler who ran to Jesus, knelt at His feet, and, with genuine sincerity, asked the Master, "What shall I do that I may inherit eternal life?" After reviewing a long list of commandments this fellow had faithfully kept, Jesus told the man to sell all his belongings, give the proceeds to the poor, take up his cross, and follow Him. The boldness of this directive caused the young ruler—in spite of his expensive sandals—to get cold feet, and he went away sorrowing because, the scripture says, "he had great possessions."[1]

Obviously, this is an important cautionary tale about the uses of wealth and the needs of the poor. But ultimately it is a story about wholehearted, unreserved devotion to divine responsibility. With or without riches, each of us is to come to Christ with the same uncompromised commitment to His gospel that was expected of this young man. In the vernacular of today's youth, we are to declare ourselves "all in."[2]

In his characteristically memorable prose, C. S. Lewis imagines the Lord saying to us something like this: "I don't want . . . your time . . . [or] your money . . . [or] your work [as much as] I [just] want You. [That tree you are pruning.] I don't want to cut off a branch here and a branch there, I want . . . the whole [thing] down. [And that tooth.] I don't want to drill [it], or crown it, or [fill] it. [I want] to have it out. [In fact, I want you to] hand over [to me your] whole natural self. . . . [And] I will give you a new self instead. In fact, I will give you Myself: my . . . will shall become [your will]."[3]

All who speak in this general conference will all be saying, one way or another, what Christ said to this rich young man: "Come unto your Savior. Come completely and wholeheartedly. Take up your cross, however heavy it may be, and follow Him."[4] They will say this knowing that in the kingdom of God, there can be no half-way measures, no starting and stopping, no turning back. To those who requested permission to bury a deceased parent or to at least say goodbye to other family members, Jesus's reply was demanding and unequivocal. "Leave that to others," He said. "No man, having put his hand to the plough, and looking back, is fit for the kingdom of God."[5] When difficult things are asked of us, even things contrary to the longings of our heart, remember that the loyalty we pledge to the cause of Christ is to be the supreme devotion of our lives. Although Isaiah reassures us it is available "without money and without price"[6]—and it is—we must be prepared, using T. S. Eliot's line, to have it cost "not less than everything."[7]

Of course, we all have some habits or flaws or personal history that could keep us from complete spiritual immersion in this work. But God is our Father and is exceptionally good at forgiving and forgetting sins we have forsaken, perhaps because we give Him so much practice in doing so. In any case, there is divine help for every one of us at any hour we feel to make a change in our behavior. God gave Saul "another heart."[8] Ezekiel called on all of ancient Israel to cast off her past and "make . . . a new heart and a new spirit."[9] Alma called for a "mighty change"[10] that would cause the soul to expand, and Jesus Himself taught that "except a man be born again, he cannot see the kingdom of God."[11] Clearly the possibility of change and living at a more elevated level has always been one of the gifts of God to those who seek it.

Friends, in our present moment we find all manner of divisions and subdivisions, sets and subsets, digital tribes and political identities, with more than enough hostility to go around. Might we ask ourselves if a "higher and holier"[12] life, to use President Russell M. Nelson's phrase, is something we could seek? When doing so, we would do well to remember that stunning period in the Book of Mormon in which those people asked and answered that question so affirmatively:

"And it came to pass that there was no contention among all the people, in all the land . . . *because of the love of God which did dwell in the hearts of the people.*

"And there were no envyings, nor strifes, . . . nor any manner of lasciviousness; and surely there could not be a happier people among all the people who had been created by the hand of God.

"There were no robbers, nor murderers, neither were there Lamanites, nor any manner of -ites; but *they were in one, the children of Christ, and heirs to the kingdom of God.*

"And how blessed were they!"[13]

What is the key to this breakthrough in contented, happy living? It is embedded there in the text in one sentence: "The love of God . . . did dwell in the hearts of the people."[14] When the love of God sets the tone for our own lives, for our relationships to each other and ultimately our feeling for all humankind, then old distinctions, limiting labels, and artificial divisions begin to pass away, and peace increases. That is precisely what happened in our Book of Mormon example. No longer were there Lamanites, or Jacobites, or Josephites, or Zoramites. There were no "-ites" at all. The people had taken on just one transcendent identity. They were all, it says, to be known as "the children of Christ."[15]

Of course, we are speaking here of the first great commandment given to the human family—to love God wholeheartedly, without reservation or compromise, that is, with all our heart, might, mind, and strength.[16] This love of God is the first great *commandment* in the universe. But the first great *truth* in the universe is that *God loves us* exactly that way—wholeheartedly, without reservation or compromise, with all of *His* heart, might, mind, and strength. And when those majestic forces from His heart and ours meet without restraint, there is a veritable explosion of spiritual, moral power. Then, as Teilhard de Chardin wrote, "for [the] second time in the history of the world, man will have discovered fire."[17]

It is then, and really only then, that we can effectively keep the second great commandment in ways that are not superficial or trivial. If we love God enough to try to be fully faithful to Him, He will give us the ability, the capacity, the will, and the way to love our neighbor and ourselves. Perhaps then we will be able to say once again, "There could not be a happier people among all the people who had been created by the hand of God."[18]

Brothers and sisters, I pray we will succeed where that rich young man failed, that we will take up the cross of Christ, however demanding it may be, regardless of the issue and regardless of the cost. I bear witness that when we pledge to follow Him, the path will, one way or another, pass by way of a crown of thorns and a stark Roman cross. No matter how wealthy our young ruler was, he wasn't wealthy enough to buy his way out of a rendezvous with those symbols, and neither can we. For the blessing of receiving the greatest of all possessions—the gift of eternal life—it is little enough that we are asked to stay the course in following the High Priest of our Profession, our Day Star, Advocate, and King. I testify with obscure Amaleki of old that each of us is to "offer [our] whole souls as an offering unto him."[19] Of such determined, steadfast devotion, we sing:

> *Praise the mount; I'm fixed upon it:*
> *Mount of thy redeeming love. . . .*
> *Here's my heart, O take and seal it;*
> *Seal it for thy courts above.*[20]

In the sacred name of Jesus Christ, amen.

Notes

1. See Mark 10:17–22.
2. See Omni 1:26.
3. C. S. Lewis, *Mere Christianity* (1960), 153.
4. See Mark 10:21.
5. See Luke 9:62.
6. Isaiah 55:1.
7. "Little Gidding," in *T. S. Eliot: Collected Poems, 1909–1962* (1963), 209.
8. 1 Samuel 10:9.
9. Ezekiel 18:31.
10. See Alma 5:9–14.
11. John 3:3.
12. Russell M. Nelson, "Closing Remarks," *Ensign* or *Liahona*, Nov. 2019, 121.
13. 4 Nephi 1:13, 15–18; emphasis added.
14. 4 Nephi 1:15.
15. 4 Nephi 1:17.
16. See Mark 12:30.
17. Pierre Teilhard de Chardin, *Toward the Future* (1975), 87.
18. 4 Nephi 1:16.
19. Omni 1:26.
20. "Come, Thou Fount of Every Blessing," *Hymns* (1948), no. 70. The text was written by Robert Robinson.

COME UNTO CHRIST AND DON'T COME ALONE

BONNIE H. CORDON
Young Women General President

I recently received a letter from an inquisitive young woman. She wrote: "I am stuck. . . . I'm not sure who I am, but I feel I'm here for something grand."

Have you ever had that searching feeling, wondering if Heavenly Father knows who you are and if He needs you? My dear youth, and to all, I testify the answer is *yes*! The Lord has a plan for you. He has prepared you for this day, *right now*, to be a strength and force for good in His mighty work. We need you! It simply will not be as grand without you!

Under sacred circumstances, our beloved prophet, President Russell M. Nelson, once reminded me of two simple truths that are foundational to your grand and glorious work.

As I sat on the couch with my husband, our prophet pulled his chair over, almost knee to knee with us, and looked at me with his piercing blue eyes. I wasn't sure if my heart was racing or had completely stopped as he called me to serve as the Young Women General President. He asked a question that still echoes in my heart, "Bonnie, what's the most important thing the [youth] need to know?"

I pondered for a moment and said, "They need to know who they are."

"YES!" he exclaimed. "And they need to know their purpose."

Our Divine Identity

You are a cherished, beloved child of Heavenly Father. He loves you so perfectly that He sent His Son, Jesus Christ, to atone for you and for me.[1] The Savior's love for us is unfailing—even when we fail! Nothing can separate us from the love of God.[2] Remembering this love can help you push back the confusion of the world that tries to weaken your confidence in your divine identity and blind you of your potential.

At an FSY conference, I met two young women who had been struggling. Both young women mentioned turning to her patriarchal blessing to rediscover the Lord's love and guidance for her personally. Find your patriarchal blessing, blow off the dust if you must, but study it often. If you don't have one, get one—soon. Don't delay finding out what the Lord wants to tell you now about who you are.

Our Eternal Purpose

President Nelson's second truth spoken to us that day is to know our purpose. This is our grand and noble charge.

Many years ago, my son Tanner was about five years old when he played his first soccer game. He was thrilled!

When we arrived at the game, we realized that his team was using a regulation-size soccer goal—not some little pop-up goal but a very large net that seemed way too big for five-year-olds.

The game took on mythic proportions as I saw Tanner take the goalie position. I was so surprised. Did he really understand his purpose in guarding the net?

The whistle blew, and we became so caught up in the game we forgot all about Tanner. Suddenly one of the opposing team members got the ball and dribbled it swiftly toward him. I looked in Tanner's direction to make certain he was ready to stand his ground and defend the goal. I saw something I was not expecting.

At some point in the game, Tanner had become distracted and began weaving his left arm through the various holes in the net. Then he did the same with his right arm. Next, his left foot. Finally, his right foot. Tanner was fully entangled in the net. He had forgotten his purpose and what he had been entrusted to do.

While Tanner's soccer career didn't last long, his lesson to me that day will never fade. We all occasionally get distracted from why we are here and divert our energies somewhere else. One of Satan's most powerful weapons is to distract us with good and better causes which, in times of need, may blind and bind us away from the best cause—the very work that called us into this world.[3]

9

Our eternal purpose is to come unto Christ and actively join Him in His great work. It is as simple as doing what President Nelson taught: "Anytime we do anything that helps anyone . . . make and keep their covenants with God, we are helping to gather Israel."[4] And when we do His work together with Him, we come to know and love Him more.

We continually seek to draw closer to the Savior through faith, cherished repentance, and keeping the commandments. As we bind ourselves to Him through covenants and ordinances, our lives are filled with confidence,[5] protection,[6] and deep and lasting joy.[7]

As we come to Him, we see others through His eyes.[8] Come unto Christ. Come now, *but don't come alone!*[9]

The gospel of Jesus Christ is not just *nice*; it is *essential* for all. "There is no other way or means whereby [we] can be saved, only in and through Christ."[10] We need Jesus Christ! The world needs Jesus Christ.[11]

Remember, the best way for you to improve the world is to prepare the world for Christ by inviting all to follow Him.

There is a story in the Book of Mormon that speaks powerfully of the resurrected Savior spending time with the Nephites. Can you imagine what that would be like?

As Christ announced that He must return to the Father, "he cast his eyes *round about again*."[12] Seeing tears in the people's eyes, He knew their hearts were longing for Him to linger.

He asked: "Have ye any that are sick among you? Bring them hither. Have ye any that are lame, or blind, . . . deaf, or that are afflicted in any manner? Bring them hither and I will heal them."[13]

Having great compassion, He set no limits and called for all "that are afflicted in any manner." I love that nothing is too big or too small for Jesus Christ to heal.

He knows *our* suffering as well and calls, Bring forth the anxious and depressed, the weary, the prideful and misunderstood, the lonely, or those who "are afflicted in any manner."

And all "did go forth . . . ; and he did heal them every one. . . .

". . . Both they who had been healed and they who were whole, [did] bow down at his feet, and did worship him."[14]

Every time I read this, I ask myself: Who will I bring to Christ? Who will *you* bring?

Can we look *round about again*, as Jesus did, to make sure no one is missed and everyone is invited to come to know Him?

Let me share an example of how simple it can be. My 15-year-old friend Peyton had a goal to read five verses of scripture at breakfast each day, but she didn't do it alone. Looking again, Peyton invited her parents and siblings, even her five-year-old brother. This seemingly small act is what Christ was teaching when He invited, "Bring them hither."

This invitation from the Lord is still extended today. Young women and young men, start now, in your own home. Will you pray and ask Heavenly Father how *you* can support *your parents* as they continue to come unto Christ? They need you just as much as you need them.

Then *look again* at your siblings, friends, and neighbors. Who will you bring to Christ?

Our Savior declared, "Behold I am the light; I have set an example for you."[15] We will feel the love and peace of the Savior as we join Him in saving God's family, for He has promised, "He that followeth me shall not walk in darkness, but shall have the light of life."[16]

What a glorious time to be engaged in the cause of Christ!

Yes, you are here for *something grand*. I join with President Nelson, who said: "The Lord needs you to change the world. As you accept and follow His will for you, you will find yourself accomplishing the impossible!"[17]

I boldly testify that the Lord knows who you are and He loves you! Together, we will advance His purpose until that great day when Christ Himself returns to this earth and calls each of us to come "hither." We will joyfully gather together, for we are those who come unto Christ, and we do not come alone. In the name of Jesus Christ, amen.

Notes

1. See John 3:16.
2. See Romans 8:32, 35–36.
3. See 1 Peter 5:8; Jeffrey R. Holland, "Sanctify Yourselves," *Ensign*, Nov. 2000, 38–40; *Liahona*, Jan. 2001, 46–49.
4. Russell M. Nelson, "Let God Prevail," *Ensign* or *Liahona*, Nov. 2020, 92–93.
5. See Doctrine and Covenants 121:45.
6. See 3 Nephi 4:10.
7. See Doctrine and Covenants 18:13, 15.
8. See W. Craig Zwick, "Lord, Wilt Thou Cause That My Eyes May Be Opened," *Ensign* or *Liahona*, Nov. 2017, 97–99.
9. See Russell M. Nelson, "Let God Prevail," 92–95.
10. Alma 38:9.
11. See Doctrine and Covenants 123:12–14.
12. 3 Nephi 17:5; emphasis added.
13. 3 Nephi 17:7.
14. 3 Nephi 17:9–10.
15. 3 Nephi 18:16.
16. John 8:12.
17. Russell M. Nelson, *Accomplishing the Impossible: What God Does, What We Can Do* (2015), 147.

THE SAVIOR'S ABIDING COMPASSION

ELDER ULISSES SOARES
Of the Quorum of the Twelve Apostles

One of the most striking principles taught by the Savior during His earthly ministry was treating others with compassion. Let us reflect on this principle and its practical application by considering the account of Jesus's visit to the home of Simon the Pharisee.

The Gospel of Luke relates that a certain woman, considered a sinner, entered Simon's home while Jesus was there. In humble contrition, the woman approached Jesus, washed His feet with her tears, wiped them with her hair, and then kissed and anointed them with a special ointment.[1] The proud host, who considered himself morally superior to the woman, thought to himself with reproach and arrogance, "This man, if he were a prophet, would have known who and what manner of woman this is that toucheth him: for she is a sinner."[2]

The Pharisee's holier-than-thou attitude led him to judge unjustly both Jesus and the woman. But in His omniscience, the Savior knew Simon's mind and, in great wisdom, challenged Simon's condescending attitude, as well as admonished him for his lack of courtesy in receiving a special guest like the Savior into his home. In fact, Jesus's direct rebuke of the Pharisee served as a witness that Jesus indeed possessed the gift of prophecy and that this woman, with a humble and contrite heart, was repentant and forgiven for her sins.[3]

As do many other events during Jesus's earthly ministry, this account demonstrates once more that the Savior acted compassionately toward all who would come unto Him—without distinction—and most especially toward those who most needed His help. The contrition and reverent love shown to Jesus by the woman were evidence of her sincere repentance and desire to receive a remission of her sins. However, Simon's superiority complex, coupled with his hardened heart,[4] prevented him from showing empathy for that repentant soul, and he referred even to the Savior of the world with indifference and contempt. His attitude revealed that his way of life was nothing more than a strict and hollow observance of rules and outward manifestations of his convictions through self-aggrandizement and false holiness.[5]

The compassionate and personalized ministering of Jesus in this account demonstrates a perfect model of how we should interact with our neighbor. The scriptures have countless examples of how the Savior, moved by His deep and abiding compassion, interacted with people of His day and helped those who were suffering and those who had "fainted, and were scattered abroad, as sheep having no shepherd."[6] He extended His merciful hand to those who needed relief from their burdens, both physically and spiritually.[7]

The compassionate attitude of Jesus is rooted in charity,[8] namely, in His pure and perfect love, which is the essence of His atoning sacrifice. Compassion is a fundamental characteristic of those who strive for sanctification, and this divine quality intertwines with other Christian traits such as mourning with those who mourn and having empathy, mercy, and kindness.[9] The expression of compassion for others is, in fact, the essence of the gospel of Jesus Christ and a marked evidence of our spiritual and emotional closeness to the Savior. Furthermore, it shows the level of influence He has on our way of life and demonstrates the magnitude of our spirits.

It is meaningful to observe that Jesus's compassionate acts were not occasional or mandated manifestations based on a list of tasks to be completed but everyday expressions of the reality of His pure love for God and His children and His abiding desire to help them.

Jesus was able to identify people's needs even at a distance. Thus, it is not surprising, for example, that immediately after healing a certain centurion's servant,[10] Jesus traveled from Capernaum to the city called Nain. It was there that Jesus performed one of the most tender miracles of His earthly ministry when He commanded a dead young man, the only son of a widowed mother, to rise and live. Jesus sensed not only the intense suffering of that poor mother but also the difficult circumstances of her life, and He was moved by genuine compassion for her.[11]

Just like the sinful woman and the widow of Nain, many people within our circle of influence are seeking comfort, attention, inclusion, and any help that we can offer them. We all can be instruments in the Lord's hands and act compassionately toward those in need, just as Jesus did.

I know a little girl who was born with very serious cleft lips and a cleft palate. She had to have the first of a series of many surgeries on the second day of her life. Moved by a genuine compassion for those who experience this same challenge, this girl and her parents seek to give support, understanding, and emotional assistance to others who face this difficult reality. They wrote to me recently and shared: "Through our daughter's challenge, we had the opportunity to meet wonderful people who needed comfort, support, and encouragement. Some time ago, our daughter, who is 11 years old now, talked with the parents of a baby with the same challenge. During this conversation, our daughter momentarily took off the mask she was wearing due to the pandemic so the parents could see that there is hope, even though that baby still has a long way to go in the next few years to fix the problem. We feel very grateful for the opportunity to extend our empathy to those who suffer, as the Savior does for us. We feel we ease our pain every time we relieve someone else's pain."

My dear friends, as we intentionally strive to incorporate a compassionate attitude into our way of life, as exemplified by the Savior, we will become more sensitive to people's needs. With that increased sensitivity, feelings of genuine interest and love will permeate our every action. The Lord will recognize our efforts, and we will surely be blessed with opportunities to be instruments in His hands in softening hearts and in bringing relief to those whose "hands . . . hang down."[12]

Jesus's admonition to Simon the Pharisee also made it clear that we should never make harsh and cruel judgment of our neighbor, because we are all in need of understanding and mercy for our imperfections from our loving Heavenly Father. Wasn't this exactly what the Savior taught on another occasion when He said, "And why beholdest thou the mote that is in thy brother's eye, but considerest not the beam that is in thine own eye?"[13]

We need to consider that it is not easy to understand all the circumstances that contribute to someone's attitude or reaction. Appearances can be deceptive and oftentimes do not represent an accurate measurement of someone's behavior. Unlike you and me, Christ is capable of clearly seeing all facets of a given situation.[14] Even knowing all our weaknesses as He does, the Savior does not rashly condemn us but continues to work with us compassionately over time, helping us to remove the beam from our eye. Jesus always looks on the heart and not on the appearance.[15] He Himself declared, "Judge not according to the appearance."[16]

Now, consider the Savior's wise counsel to the twelve Nephite disciples regarding this question:

"And know ye that ye shall be judges of this people, according to the judgment which I shall give unto you, which shall be just. Therefore, what manner of men ought ye to be? Verily I say unto you, even as I am."[17]

"Therefore I would that ye should be perfect even as I, or your Father who is in heaven is perfect."[18]

In this context, the Lord fixes judgment upon those who take it upon themselves to judge the supposed shortcomings of others unrighteously. In order to qualify ourselves to make righteous judgments, we must strive to become like the Savior and look at the imperfections of individuals compassionately, even through His eyes. Considering we still have a long way to go to reach perfection, perhaps it would be better if we sit at Jesus's feet and plead for mercy for our own imperfections, as did the repentant woman in the Pharisee's house, and not spend so much time and energy fixating on the perceived imperfections of others.

My dear friends, I testify that as we strive to incorporate the Savior's compassionate example into our lives, our capacity to compliment the virtues of our neighbors will increase and our natural instinct to judge their imperfections will decrease. Our communion with God will grow, and certainly our lives will become sweeter, our feelings more tender, and we will find a never-ending source of happiness. We will be known as peacemakers,[19] whose words are as gentle as the dew of a spring morning.

I pray that we will become more long-suffering and understanding of others and that the Lord's mercy will, in perfect meekness, soothe our impatience with their imperfections. This is the Savior's invitation to us. I testify that He lives. He is the perfect model of merciful and patient discipleship. I bear my testimony of these truths in the holy name of the Savior Jesus Christ, amen.

Notes

1. See Luke 7:36–39.
2. Luke 7:39.
3. See Luke 7:40–50.
4. See 1 Nephi 17:45–46.
5. See Matthew 5:20; 16:6–12; 23; Luke 11:37–44; 18:9–14.
6. Matthew 9:36.
7. See Matthew 20:34; Mark 1:41; Luke 7:13; 3 Nephi 17:6.
8. See Guide to the Scriptures, "Charity," scriptures.ChurchofJesusChrist.org.
9. See Guide to the Scriptures, "Compassion."
10. See Luke 7:1–10.
11. See Luke 7:11–15.
12. Doctrine and Covenants 81:5.
13. Matthew 7:3.
14. See Guide to the Scriptures, "Omniscient."
15. See 1 Samuel 16:7.
16. John 7:24.
17. 3 Nephi 27:27.
18. 3 Nephi 12:48.
19. See Guide to the Scriptures, "Peacemaker."

THE LOVE OF GOD

ELDER D. TODD CHRISTOFFERSON
Of the Quorum of the Twelve Apostles

Our Heavenly Father loves us profoundly and perfectly.[1] In His love, He created a plan, a plan of redemption and happiness to open to us all the opportunities and joys we are willing to receive, up to and including all that He has and is.[2] To achieve this, He was even willing to offer His Beloved Son, Jesus Christ, as our Redeemer. "For God so loved the world, that he gave his only begotten Son, that whosoever believeth in him should not perish, but have everlasting life."[3] His is a Father's pure love—universal to all yet personal to each.

Jesus Christ shares with the Father this same perfect love. When the Father first elaborated His great plan of happiness, He called for one to act as a Savior to redeem us—an essential part of that plan. Jesus volunteered, "Here am I, send me."[4] The Savior "doeth not anything save it be for the benefit of the world; for he loveth the world, even that he layeth down his own life that he may draw all men unto him. Wherefore, he commandeth none that they shall not partake of his salvation."[5]

This divine love should give us abundant comfort and confidence as we pray to the Father in the name of Christ. Not one of us is a stranger to Them. We need not hesitate to call upon God, even when we feel unworthy. We can rely on the mercy and merits of Jesus Christ to be heard.[6] As we abide in God's love, we depend less and less on the approval of others to guide us.

The Love of God Does Not Excuse Sin; Rather, It Offers Redemption

Because God's love is all-embracing, some speak of it as "unconditional," and in their minds they may project that thought to mean that God's *blessings* are "unconditional" and that *salvation* is "unconditional." They are not. Some are wont to say, "The Savior loves me just as I am," and that is certainly true. But He cannot take any of us into His kingdom just as we are, "for no unclean thing can dwell there, or dwell in his presence."[7] Our sins must first be resolved.

Professor Hugh Nibley once noted that the kingdom of God cannot endure if it indulges even the smallest sin: "The slightest taint of corruption means that the other world would be neither incorruptible nor eternal. The tiniest flaw in a building, institution, code, or character will inevitably prove fatal in the long run of eternity."[8] The commandments of God are "strict"[9] because His kingdom and its citizens can stand only if they consistently reject evil and choose good, without exception.[10]

Elder Jeffrey R. Holland observed, "Jesus clearly understood what many in our modern culture seem to forget: that there is a crucial difference between the commandment to forgive sin (which He had an infinite capacity to do) and the warning against condoning it (which He never ever did even once)."[11]

Despite our present imperfections, however, we can still hope to attain "a name and standing,"[12] a place, in His Church and in the celestial world. After making it clear that He cannot excuse or wink at sin, the Lord assures us:

"Nevertheless, he that repents and does the commandments of the Lord shall be forgiven."[13]

"And as often as my people repent will I forgive them their trespasses against me."[14]

Repentance and divine grace resolve the dilemma:

"Remember also the words which Amulek spake unto Zeezrom, in the city of Ammonihah; for he said unto him that the Lord surely should come to redeem his people, but that he should not come to redeem them *in* their sins, but to redeem them *from* their sins.

"And he hath power given unto him from the Father to redeem them from their sins because of repentance; therefore he hath sent his angels to declare the tidings of the conditions of repentance, which bringeth unto the power of the Redeemer, unto the salvation of their souls."[15]

With the condition of repentance, the Lord can extend mercy without robbing justice, and "God ceaseth not to be God."[16]

The way of the world, as you know, is anti-Christ, or "anything but Christ." Our day is a replay of Book of Mormon history in which charismatic figures pursue unrighteous dominion over others, celebrate sexual license, and promote accumulating wealth as the object of our existence. Their philosophies "justify in committing a little sin"[17] or even a lot of sin, but none can offer redemption. That comes only through the blood of the Lamb. The best the "anything but Christ" or "anything but repentance" crowd can offer is the unfounded claim that sin does not exist or that if it exists, it ultimately has no consequences. I can't see that argument getting much traction at the Final Judgment.[18]

We don't have to attempt the impossible in trying to rationalize our sins away. And on the other hand, we don't have to attempt the impossible in erasing the effects of sin by our own merit alone. Ours is not a religion of rationalization nor a religion of perfectionism but a religion of redemption—redemption through Jesus Christ. If we are among the penitent, with His Atonement our sins are nailed to His cross, and "with his stripes we are healed."[19]

The Yearning Love of the Prophets Mirrors the Love of God

I have long been impressed by, and have also felt, the yearning love of the prophets of God in their warnings against sin. They are not motivated by a desire to condemn. Their true desire mirrors the love of God; in fact, it *is* the love of God. They love those to whom they are sent, whoever they may be and whatever they may be like. Just as the Lord, His servants do not want anyone to suffer the pains of sin and poor choices.[20]

Alma was sent to declare the message of repentance and redemption to a hate-filled people who were willing to persecute, torture, and even kill Christian believers, including Alma himself. Yet he loved them and yearned for their salvation. After declaring the Atonement of Christ to the people of Ammonihah, Alma pleaded: "And now, my brethren, *I wish from the inmost part of my heart, yea, with great anxiety even unto pain,* that ye would hearken unto my words, and cast off your sins, . . . that ye may be lifted up at the last day and enter into [God's] rest."[21]

In President Russell M. Nelson's words, "It is precisely because we do care deeply about all of God's children that we proclaim His truth."[22]

God Loves You; Do You Love Him?

The love of the Father and the Son is freely given but also includes hopes and expectations. Again, quoting President Nelson, "God's laws are motivated entirely by His infinite love for us and His desire for us to become all we can become."[23]

Because They love you, They do not want to leave you "just as you are." Because They love you, They want you to have joy and success. Because They love you, They want you to repent because that is the path to happiness. But it is your choice—They honor your agency. You must choose to love Them, to serve Them, to keep Their commandments. Then They can more abundantly *bless* you as well as *love* you.

Their principal expectation of us is that we also love. "He that loveth not knoweth not God; for God is love."[24] As John wrote, "Beloved, if God so loved us, we ought also to love one another."[25]

Former Primary General President Joy D. Jones recalled that as a young couple, she and her husband were called to visit and minister to a family who hadn't been to church for many years. It was immediately clear in their first visit that they were not wanted. After the frustration of additional failed attempts, and after much sincere prayer and pondering, Brother and Sister Jones received an answer to the *why* of their service in this verse from the Doctrine and Covenants: "Thou shalt love the Lord thy God with all thy heart, with all thy might, mind, and strength; and in the name of Jesus Christ *thou shalt serve him.*"[26] Sister Jones said:

"We realized that we were sincerely striving to serve this family and to serve our bishop, but we had to ask ourselves if we were really serving out of love for the Lord. . . .

". . . We began looking forward to our visits with this dear family because of our love for the Lord [see 1 Nephi 11:22]. We were doing it for Him. He made the struggle no longer a struggle. After many months of our standing on the doorstep, the family began letting us in. Eventually, we had regular prayer and tender gospel discussions together. A long-lasting friendship developed. We were worshipping and loving Him by loving His children."[27]

In acknowledging that God loves us perfectly, we each might ask, "How well do I love God? Can He rely on my love as I rely on His?" Would it not be a worthy aspiration to live so that God can love us not just *in spite of* our failings but also *because of* what we are becoming? Oh, that He could say of you and me as He said of Hyrum Smith, for example, "I, the Lord, love him because of the integrity of his heart."[28] Let us remember John's kind admonition: "For this is the love of God, that we keep his commandments: and his commandments are not grievous."[29]

Indeed, His commandments are not grievous—just the opposite. They mark the path of healing, happiness, peace, and joy. Our Father and our Redeemer have blessed us with commandments, and in obeying Their commandments, we feel Their perfect love more fully and more profoundly.[30]

Here is the solution for our incessantly quarrelsome times—the love of God. In the golden age of Book of Mormon history following the Savior's ministry, it is reported that "there was *no contention* in the land, *because of the love of God* which did dwell in the hearts of the people."[31] As we strive toward Zion, remember the promise in Revelation: "Blessed are they that do his commandments, that they may have right to the tree of life, and may enter in through the gates into the [holy] city."[32]

I bear witness of the reality of our Heavenly Father and our Redeemer, Jesus Christ, and of Their constant, undying love. In the name of Jesus Christ, amen.

Notes

1. In preparing this message, I have drawn upon principles taught by President Russell M. Nelson in "The Love and Laws of God" (Brigham Young University devotional, Sept. 17, 2019), speeches.byu.edu, and by President Dallin H. Oaks in "Love and Law," *Ensign* or *Liahona*, Nov. 2009, 26–29.

2. See Moses 1:39.

3. John 3:16.

4. Abraham 3:27.

5. 2 Nephi 26:24. As Jesus Himself said: "Greater love hath no man than this, that a man lay down his life for his friends. Ye are my friends, if ye do whatsoever I command you" (John 15:13–14).

6. See 2 Nephi 2:8; Moroni 6:4.

7. Moses 6:57.

8. *Temple and Cosmos: Beyond This Ignorant Present*, vol. 12 of The Collected Works of Hugh Nibley (1992), 61; see also *Approaching Zion*, vol. 9 of The Collected Works of Hugh Nibley (1989), 274: "It [an everlasting Zion] can no more carry on forever laden with defects and imperfections than a bridge or tower can stand forever weakened by even minor flaws in construction."

9. Alma 37:13.

10. Thus, the Savior declares: "Strait is the gate, and narrow is the way, which leadeth unto life" (Matthew 7:14) and "I the Lord cannot look upon sin with the least degree of allowance" (Doctrine and Covenants 1:31; see also Alma 45:16).

11. Jeffrey R. Holland, "The Cost—and Blessings—of Discipleship," *Ensign* or *Liahona*, May 2014, 8; see also Jeffrey R. Holland, "The Second Half of the Second Century of Brigham Young University" (university conference address, Aug. 23, 2021), 4, speeches.byu.edu: "As near as I can tell, Christ never *once* withheld His love from anyone, but He also never once said to anyone, 'Because I love you, you are exempt from keeping my commandments.'"

12. Doctrine and Covenants 109:24.

13. Doctrine and Covenants 1:32.

14. Mosiah 26:30.

15. Helaman 5:10–11; emphasis added.

16. Alma 42:23; see also verses 13–15, 22, 24–25.

17. 2 Nephi 28:8.

18. See 2 Nephi 9:46.

19. Isaiah 53:5; see also Mosiah 14:5.

20. See Mosiah 28:3.

21. Alma 13:27, 29; emphasis added.

22. Russell M. Nelson, "The Love and Laws of God," 3.

23. Russell M. Nelson, "The Love and Laws of God," 3.

24. 1 John 4:8.

25. 1 John 4:11.

26. Doctrine and Covenants 59:5; emphasis added.

27. Joy D. Jones, "For Him," *Ensign* or *Liahona*, Nov. 2018, 50.

28. Doctrine and Covenants 124:15.

29. 1 John 5:3; see also John 14:15; 2 John 1:6.

30. See John 15:10.

31. 4 Nephi 1:15; emphasis added.

32. Revelation 22:14.

BECOMING MORE IN CHRIST: THE PARABLE OF THE SLOPE

ELDER CLARK G. GILBERT
Of the Seventy

As a young boy, I had great aspirations. One day after school, I asked, "Mom, what should I be when I grow up: a professional basketball player or a rock star?" Unfortunately, Clark "the toothless wonder" showed no signs of future athletic or musical glory. And despite multiple efforts, I was repeatedly denied admission to my school's advanced academic program. My teachers finally suggested I should just stick to the standard classroom. Over time, I developed compensating study habits. But it wasn't until my mission to Japan that I felt my intellectual and spiritual possibilities begin to emerge. I continued to work hard. But for the first time in my life, I systematically involved the Lord in my development, and it made all the difference.

Brothers and sisters, in this Church, we believe in the divine potential of all of God's children and in our ability to become something more in Christ. In the Lord's timing, it is not where we start but where we are headed that matters most.[1]

To demonstrate this principle, I will draw on some basic math. Now, don't panic at hearing the word *math* in general conference. Our BYU–Idaho math faculty assure me that even the beginner will grasp this central concept. It starts with the formula for a line. The intercept, for our purposes, is the beginning of our line. The intercept can have either a high or a low starting point. The slope of the line can then be positively or negatively inclined.

We all have different intercepts in life—we start in different places with different life endowments. Some are born with high intercepts, full of opportunity. Others face beginning circumstances that are challenging and seem unfair.[2] We then progress along a slope of personal progress. Our future will be determined far less by our starting point and much more by our slope. Jesus Christ sees divine potential no matter where we start. He saw it in the beggar, the sinner, and the infirm. He saw it in the fisherman, the tax collector, and even the zealot. No matter where we start, Christ considers what we do with what we are given.[3] While the world focuses on our intercept, God focuses on our slope. In the Lord's calculus, He will do everything He can to help us turn our slopes toward heaven.

This principle should give comfort to those who struggle, and *pause* to those who seem to have every advantage. Let me start by addressing individuals with difficult starting circumstances, including poverty, limited access to education, and challenging family situations. Others face physical challenges, mental health constraints, or strong genetic predispositions.[4] For any struggling with difficult starting points, please recognize that the Savior knows our struggles. He took "upon him [our] infirmities, that his bowels [might] be filled with mercy, . . . that he [might] know . . . how to succor [us] according to [our] infirmities."[5]

Let me share two areas of encouragement for those facing difficult starting circumstances. First, focus on where you are headed and not where you began. It would be wrong to ignore your circumstances—they are real and need to be addressed. But overfocusing on a difficult starting point can cause it to define you and even *constrain* your ability to choose.[6]

Years ago I served with a group of inner-city youth in Boston, Massachusetts, who were largely new to the gospel and to the expectations of the Church. It was tempting to confuse my empathy and concern for their situation with a desire to lower God's standards.[7] I eventually realized that the most powerful way to show my love was to never lower my expectations. With everything I knew to do, we focused together on their potential, and each of them began to elevate their slopes. Their growth in the gospel was gradual but steady. Today they have served missions, have graduated from college, have been married in the temple, and are leading remarkable personal and professional lives.

Second, involve the Lord in the process of lifting your slope. While serving as the president of BYU–Pathway Worldwide, I remember sitting in a large devotional in Lima, Peru, where Elder

Carlos A. Godoy was the speaker. As he looked out over the congregation, he seemed overwhelmed observing so many faithful first-generation university students. Perhaps reflecting on his own path through such difficult circumstances, Elder Godoy stated emotionally: the Lord will "help you more than you can help yourself. [So] involve the Lord in this process."[8] The prophet Nephi taught "that it is by grace that we are saved, after all we can do."[9] We must do our best,[10] which includes repentance, but it is only through the Lord's grace that we can realize our divine potential.[11]

Finally, let me share two areas of counsel for those with elevated starting points. First, can we show some humility for circumstances we may not have created ourselves? As former BYU president Rex E. Lee quoted to his students, "We have all drunk from wells we did not dig, and warmed ourselves by fires we did not build."[12] He then called on his students to give back and replenish the educational wells that earlier pioneers had built. Failure to reseed the fields planted by others can be the equivalent of returning a talent without increase.

Second, focusing on a high starting point can often trap us into feeling that we are thriving when in fact our inner slope may be quite stagnant. Harvard professor Clayton M. Christensen taught that the most successful people are the humblest because they are confident enough to be corrected by and learn from anyone.[13] Elder D. Todd Christofferson counseled us to "willingly [find ways] to accept and even seek correction."[14] Even when things appear to be going well, we must seek out opportunities to improve through prayerful petition.

Regardless of whether we start in abundant or difficult circumstances, we will realize our ultimate potential only when we make God our partner. I recently had a conversation with a nationally prominent educator who was inquiring about the success of BYU–Pathway. He was bright and his inquiry was sincere, but he clearly wanted a secular response. I shared with him our retention programs and mentoring efforts. But I concluded by saying, "These are all good practices, but the real reason our students are progressing is because we teach them their divine potential. Imagine if your whole life, you were told you could never succeed. Then consider the impact of being taught that you are an actual son or daughter of God with divine possibility." He paused, then replied simply, "That's powerful."

Brothers and sisters, one of the miracles of this, the Lord's Church, is that each of us can become something more in Christ. I know of no other organization that gives its members more opportunities to serve, give back, repent, and become better people. Whether we start in abundant or difficult circumstances, let us keep our sights and our slopes pointed heavenward. As we do, Christ will lift us to a higher place. In the name of Jesus Christ, amen.

Notes

1. See Clark G. Gilbert, "The Mismeasure of Man" (BYU–Pathway Worldwide devotional, Jan. 12, 2021), byupathway.org/speeches. In this message I explored how the world often mismeasures human potential. Even well-meaning individuals who draw on the important work of leading psychologists who advocate concepts of grit (Angela Duckworth) and growth mindset (Carol S. Dweck) underestimate real human capacity when they rely only on learned patterns and ignore our divine potential in Christ.
2. See Dale G. Renlund, "Infuriating Unfairness," *Liahona*, May 2021, 41–45.
3. See Matthew 25:14–30. In the parable of the talents, each servant received a different number of talents from their master. But judgment wasn't determined by what they received but by how it was managed. It was the *increase* that led the Lord to say, "Well done, thou good and faithful servant: thou hast been faithful over a few things, I will make thee ruler over many things" (Matthew 25:21).
4. See Mosiah 3:19. One implication may be that our exposure to the pull of the natural man may be different given different genetic predispositions. Just as we are each endowed with different gifts, we also have different physical, mental, and emotional challenges that we must learn to manage and overcome.
5. Alma 7:11–12. Christ not only helps us overcome our sins through repentance, but He knows how to comfort us in our life's difficulties because, through the Atonement, He has felt and overcome all human suffering.
6. Elder David A. Bednar reminds us that we are agents and must act for ourselves. When we define ourselves by the labels of the world, we limit our divine potential and, in so doing, limit our ability to choose. (See David A. Bednar, "And Nothing Shall Offend Them," *Ensign* or *Liahona*, Nov. 2006, 89–92.)
7. See Russell M. Nelson, "The Love and Laws of God" (Brigham Young University devotional, Sept. 17, 2019), speeches.byu.edu. In this BYU devotional, President Nelson teaches that *because* God and His Son love us, They have given us laws and expectations that will help us. "God's laws reflect His perfect love for each of us. His laws keep us spiritually safe and help us to progress eternally" (page 2).
8. Carlos A. Godoy, BYU–Pathway Connections Conference, Lima, Peru, May 3, 2018.
9. 2 Nephi 25:23.
10. My parents established an extended Gilbert family motto to "DO YOUR BEST." Another way to frame the parable of the slope is to emphasize that if we do our best, we can trust God to step in and make up the difference.
11. See Clark G. Gilbert, "From Grit to Grace" (BYU–Pathway Worldwide devotional, Sept. 25, 2018), byupathway.org/speeches. In this message I explore the idea that even though we must

learn to work hard and develop effective patterns of discipline, to realize our true potential in Jesus Christ, we must learn to draw on His grace.

12. Rex E. Lee, "Some Thoughts about Butterflies, Replenishment, Environmentalism, and Ownership" (Brigham Young University devotional, Sept. 15, 1992), 2, speeches.byu.edu; see also Deuteronomy 6:11.
13. See Clayton M. Christensen, "How Will You Measure Your Life?," *Harvard Business Review*, July–Aug. 2010, hbr.org. This message was originally given as a Class Day address tied to Harvard Business School graduation. In his message, Professor Christensen cautioned his students not to decouple confidence from humility, reminding them that to continue to progress throughout life, they would need to be humble enough to seek correction and learn from others.
14. D. Todd Christofferson, "As Many as I Love, I Rebuke and Chasten," *Ensign* or *Liahona*, May 2011, 97.

A FAITHFUL SEARCH REWARDED

ELDER PATRICIO M. GIUFFRA
Of the Seventy

Beginning in 1846, thousands of pioneer men, women, and children headed westward to Zion. Their great faith stirred their boundless courage. For some, that trip was never finished as they died along the way. Others, facing great adversity, pressed forward in faith.

Because of them, generations later, my family enjoyed the blessings of the true gospel of Jesus Christ.

Much like another young man, whom I will mention later, I was 14 when I started to question religion and my faith. I attended the church of another denomination close to my house, but I felt the desire to visit many different churches.

One afternoon, I noticed two young men in dark suits and white shirts entering my neighbor's home. These young men looked—special.

The next day I met my neighbor, Leonor Lopez, and asked her about those two men. Leonor explained that they were missionaries for The Church of Jesus Christ of Latter-day Saints. She joyfully told me that her family was baptized into the Church a year earlier. Seeing my interest, Leonor invited me to meet the missionaries and learn about the Church.

Two days later, I joined the Lopez family to meet the missionaries. They introduced themselves as Elder John Messerly from Ogden, Utah, and Elder Christopher Osorio from Walnut Creek, California. I will never forget them.

Since I was only 14, Elder Messerly insisted we go next door to my home so that my mother could know what they were teaching me. There, he kindly explained that they came to share a message about Jesus Christ and asked for her permission to teach me. Mother agreed and even joined us while they taught me.

The missionaries first asked Leonor to offer a prayer. This touched me very deeply because her prayer was not a repetition of memorized words but an expression from her heart. I felt she was really talking to her Heavenly Father.

The missionaries then taught us about Jesus Christ. They showed a picture of Him that impressed me because it was a picture of the resurrected, living Christ.

They continued, teaching us how Jesus established His Church in ancient times, with Him at the head joined by twelve Apostles. They taught us about the Apostasy—how truth and Christ's authority had been taken from the earth after His Apostles died.

They told us of a young 14-year-old boy named Joseph Smith who, during the early 1800s, visited different churches searching for truth. As time went on, Joseph became even more confused. After reading in the Bible that we can "ask of God"[1] for wisdom, Joseph, acting in faith, retired to a grove of trees to pray and ask which church he should join.

One of the missionaries read Joseph's account of what happened as he prayed:

"I saw a pillar of light exactly over my head, above the brightness of the sun, which descended gradually until it fell upon me.

". . . When the light rested upon me I saw two Personages, whose brightness and glory defy all description, standing above me in the air. One of them spake unto me, calling me by name and said, pointing to the other—*This is My Beloved Son. Hear Him!*"[2]

During that lesson, the Spirit confirmed to me several truths.

First, God listens to all His children's sincere prayers, and heaven is open to all—not just a few.

Second, God the Father, Jesus Christ, and the Holy Ghost are three separate beings, united in Their purpose "to bring to pass the immortality and eternal life of man."[3]

Third, we are created in the image of God. Our Heavenly Father and His Son, Jesus Christ, have bodies of flesh and bones like us, but They are glorified and perfected, and the Holy Ghost is a personage of spirit.[4]

Fourth, through Joseph Smith, Jesus Christ restored His gospel and true Church to the earth. The priesthood authority conferred on Christ's Apostles 2,000 years ago is the same priesthood conferred upon Joseph Smith and Oliver Cowdery by Peter, James, and John.[5]

Finally, we learned about another testament of Jesus Christ: the Book of Mormon. Written by ancient prophets, it tells of the people who lived in the Americas before, during, and after the birth of Jesus. From it we learn of how they knew, loved, and worshipped Christ, who appeared to them as the resurrected Savior.

The Spirit moved me profoundly as I learned of the Savior's declaration to them: "Behold, I am Jesus Christ, whom the prophets testified shall come into the world."[6]

The missionaries gave us our own copy of the Book of Mormon. We read and accepted the invitation found at the end of the Book of Mormon, which reads:

"And when ye shall receive these things, I would exhort you that ye would ask God, the Eternal Father, in the name of Christ, if these things are not true; and if ye shall ask with a sincere heart, with real intent, having faith in Christ, he will manifest the truth of it unto you, by the power of the Holy Ghost.

"And by the power of the Holy Ghost ye may know the truth of all things."[7]

It has been almost 45 years since my mother and I first learned the joy and power of having faith in Christ. It was because of their faith in Christ that the Lopez family shared their new faith with me. It was because of their faith in Christ that these two missionaries left their homes in the United States to find my mother and me. It was the faith of all these dear friends that planted a mustard seed of faith in us that has since grown into a mighty tree of eternal blessings.

During these blessed years, we have known, as President Russell M. Nelson declared: "Everything good in life—every potential blessing of eternal significance—begins with faith. Allowing God to prevail in our lives begins with faith that He is willing to guide us. True repentance begins with faith that Jesus Christ has the power to cleanse, heal, and strengthen us."[8]

I invite us all to continually increase our faith in Christ, who has changed the lives of my beloved mother and me and continues to change the lives of all who seek Him. I know that Joseph Smith is the Prophet of the Restoration, that President Nelson is our prophet today, that Jesus is the living Christ and our Redeemer, and that Heavenly Father lives and answers all His children's prayers. I testify of these truths in the sacred name of Jesus Christ, amen.

Notes

1. James 1:5.
2. Joseph Smith—History 1:16–17.
3. Moses 1:39.
4. See Genesis 1:26; Doctrine and Covenants 130:22.
5. See Doctrine and Covenants 27:12.
6. 3 Nephi 11:10.
7. Moroni 10:4–5.
8. Russell M. Nelson, "Christ Is Risen; Faith in Him Will Move Mountains," *Liahona*, May 2021, 102.

THE NEED FOR A CHURCH

PRESIDENT DALLIN H. OAKS

First Counselor in the First Presidency

Many years ago, Elder Mark E. Petersen, a member of the Quorum of the Twelve Apostles, began a talk with this example:

"Kenneth and his wife, Lucille, are good people, honest and upright. They don't go to church, though, and they feel they can be good enough without it. They teach their children honesty and virtue and they tell themselves that is about all the Church would do for them.

"And, anyway, they insist that they need their weekends for family recreation . . . [and] church-going would really get in their way."[1]

Today, my message concerns such good and religious-minded people who have stopped attending or participating in their churches.[2] When I say "churches," I include synagogues, mosques, or other religious organizations. We are concerned that attendance in all of these is down significantly, nationwide.[3] If we cease valuing our churches for any reason, we threaten our personal spiritual life, and significant numbers separating themselves from God reduce His blessings to our nations.

Attendance and activity in a church help us become better people and better influences on the lives of others. In church we are taught how to apply religious principles. We learn from one another. A persuasive example is more powerful than a sermon. We are strengthened by associating with others of like minds. In church attendance and participation, our hearts are, as the Bible says, "knit together in love."[4]

I.

The scriptures God has given Christians in the Bible and in modern revelation clearly teach the need for a church. Both show that Jesus Christ organized a church and contemplated that a church would carry on His work after Him. He called Twelve Apostles and gave them authority and keys to direct it. The Bible teaches that

Christ is "the head of the church"[5] and that its officers were given "for the perfecting of the saints, for the work of the ministry, for the edifying of the body of Christ."[6] Surely the Bible is clear on the origin of a church and the need for it now.

Some say that attending church meetings is not helping them. Some say, "I didn't learn anything today" or "No one was friendly to me" or "I was offended." Personal disappointments should never keep us from the doctrine of Christ, who taught us to serve, not to be served.[7] With this in mind, another member described the focus of his Church attendance:

"Years ago, I changed my attitude about going to church. No longer do I go to church for my sake, but to think of others. I make a point of saying hello to people who sit alone, to welcome visitors, . . . to volunteer for an assignment. . . .

"In short, I go to church each week with the intent of being active, not passive, and making a positive difference in people's lives."[8]

President Spencer W. Kimball taught that "we do not go to Sabbath meetings to be entertained or even solely to be instructed. We go to worship the Lord. It is an individual responsibility. . . . If the service is a failure to you, you have failed. No one can worship for you; you must do your own waiting upon the Lord."[9]

Church attendance can open our hearts and sanctify our souls.

In a church we don't just serve alone or by our own choice or at our convenience. We usually serve in a team. In service we find heaven-sent opportunities to rise above the individualism of our age. Church-directed service helps us overcome the personal selfishness that can retard our spiritual growth.

There are other important advantages to mention, even briefly. In church we associate with wonderful people striving to serve God. This reminds us that we are not alone in our religious activities. We all need associations with others, and church associations are some of the best we can experience, for us and our companions and children. Without those associations, especially between children and faithful parents, research shows increasing difficulty for parents to raise children in their faith.[10]

II.

So far, I have spoken about churches generally. Now I address the special reasons for membership, attendance, and participation in the Savior's restored Church of Jesus Christ of Latter-day Saints.

We, of course, affirm that the scriptures, ancient and modern, clearly teach the origin and need for a church directed by and with the authority of our Lord, Jesus Christ. We also testify that the restored Church of Jesus Christ has been established to teach the fulness of His doctrine and to officiate with His priesthood authority to perform the ordinances necessary to enter the kingdom of God.[11] Members who forgo Church attendance and rely only on individual spirituality separate themselves from these gospel essentials: the power and blessings of the priesthood, the fulness of restored doctrine, and the motivations and opportunities to apply that doctrine. They forfeit their opportunity to qualify to perpetuate their family for eternity.

Another great advantage of the restored Church is that it helps us grow spiritually. Growth means change. In spiritual terms this means repenting and seeking to draw nearer to the Lord. In the restored Church we have doctrine, procedures, and inspired helpers that assist us to repent. Their purpose, even in membership councils, is not punishment, like the outcome of a criminal court. Church membership councils lovingly seek to help us qualify for the mercy of forgiveness made possible through the Atonement of Jesus Christ.

Individual spirituality can seldom provide the motivation and structure for unselfish service provided by the restored Church. Great examples of this are the young men and women and seniors who put aside their schooling or retirement activities to accept missionary callings. They work as missionaries to strangers in unfamiliar places they have not chosen. The same is true of faithful members who participate in the unselfish service we call "temple work." None of such service would be possible without the Church that sponsors it, organizes it, and directs it.

Our members' religious faith and Church service have taught them how to work in cooperative efforts to benefit the larger community. That kind of experience and development does not happen in the individualism so prevalent in the practices of our current society. In the geographic organization of our local wards, we associate and work with persons we might not otherwise have chosen, persons who teach us and test us.

In addition to helping us learn spiritual qualities like love, compassion, forgiveness, and patience, this gives us the opportunities to learn how to work with persons of very different backgrounds and preferences. This advantage has helped many of our members, and many organizations are blessed by their participation. Latter-day Saints are renowned for their ability to lead and unite in cooperative efforts. That tradition originated with our courageous pioneers who colonized the Intermountain West and established our valued tradition of unselfish cooperation for the common good.

Most humanitarian and charitable efforts need to be accomplished by pooling and managing individual resources on a large scale. The restored Church does this with its enormous humanitarian efforts worldwide. These include distributing educational and medical supplies, feeding the hungry, caring for refugees, helping to reverse the effects of addictions, and a host of others. Our Church members are renowned for their Helping Hands projects in natural disasters. Church membership allows us to be part of such large-scale efforts. Members also pay fast offerings to help the poor in their own midst.

In addition to feeling peace and joy through the companionship of the Spirit, our Church-attending members enjoy the fruits of gospel living, such as the blessings of living the Word of Wisdom and the material and spiritual prosperity promised for living the law of tithing. We also have the blessing of counsel from inspired leaders.

Crowning all of this are the authoritative priesthood ordinances necessary for eternity, including the sacrament we receive each Sabbath day. The culminating ordinance in the restored Church is the everlasting covenant of marriage, which makes possible the perpetuation of glorious family relationships. President Russell M.

Nelson taught this principle in a memorable way. He said: "We cannot *wish* our way into the presence of God. We are to obey the laws upon which [that blessing is] predicated."[12]

One of those laws is to worship in church each Sabbath day.[13] Our worship and application of eternal principles draw us closer to God and magnify our capacity to love. Parley P. Pratt, one of the original Apostles of this dispensation, described how he felt when the Prophet Joseph Smith explained these principles: "I felt that God was my heavenly Father indeed; that Jesus was my brother, and that the wife of my bosom was an immortal, eternal companion: a kind, ministering angel, given to me as a comfort, and a crown of glory for ever and ever. In short, I could now love with the spirit and with the understanding also."[14]

In closing, I remind all that we do not believe that good can be accomplished only through a church. Independent of a church, we see millions of people supporting and carrying out innumerable good works. Individually, Latter-day Saints participate in many of them. We see these works as a manifestation of the eternal truth that "the Spirit giveth light to *every man* that cometh into the world."[15]

Despite the good works that can be accomplished without a church, the fulness of doctrine and its saving and exalting ordinances are available only in the restored Church. In addition, Church attendance gives us the strength and enhancement of faith that comes from associating with other believers and worshipping together with those who are also striving to stay on the covenant path and be better disciples of Christ. I pray that we will all be steadfast in these Church experiences as we seek eternal life, the greatest of all the gifts of God, in the name of Jesus Christ, amen.

Notes
1. Mark E. Petersen, "Eternal Togetherness," *Ensign*, Nov. 1974, 48.
2. See D. Todd Christofferson, "Why the Church," *Ensign* or *Liahona*, Nov. 2015, 108–11.
3. See Jeffrey M. Jones, "U.S. Church Membership Falls below Majority for First Time," *Gallup*, Mar. 29, 2021, news.gallup.com/poll/341963/church-membership-falls-below-majority -first-time.aspx.
4. Colossians 2:2.
5. See Ephesians 5:23–24.
6. Ephesians 4:12.
7. See James 1:27.

8. Mark Skousen to Dallin H. Oaks, Feb. 15, 2009.
9. *Teachings of Presidents of the Church: Spencer W. Kimball* (2006), 173–74.
10. See Elizabeth Weiss Ozotak, "Social and Cognitive Influences on the Development of Religious Beliefs and Commitment in Adolescence," *Journal for the Scientific Study of Religion*, vol. 28, no. 4 (Dec. 1989), 448–63.
11. See John 3:5.
12. Russell M. Nelson, "Now Is the Time to Prepare," *Ensign* or *Liahona*, May 2005, 18.
13. See Doctrine and Covenants 59:9.
14. *Autobiography of Parley P. Pratt*, ed. Parley P. Pratt Jr. (1938), 298.
15. Doctrine and Covenants 84:46; emphasis added; see also Doctrine and Covenants 58:27–28.

SATURDAY
AFTERNOON
SESSION

OCTOBER 2, 2021

WITH THE POWER OF GOD IN GREAT GLORY (1 NEPHI 14:14)

ELDER DAVID A. BEDNAR
Of the Quorum of the Twelve Apostles

I pray that the Holy Ghost will enlighten and edify all of us as we consider together the marvelous work of salvation and exaltation in the dispensation of the fulness of times.

Moroni's First Visit to Joseph Smith

Approximately three years after the First Vision, on the night of September 21, 1823, young Joseph Smith was praying to receive a remission of his sins and to know of his state and standing before God.[1] A personage appeared at his bedside, called Joseph by name, and declared "he was a messenger sent from the presence of God . . . and that his name was Moroni." He explained "that God had a work for [Joseph] to do"[2] and then instructed him about the coming forth of the Book of Mormon. Significantly, the Book of Mormon was one of the first topics addressed in Moroni's message.

The Book of Mormon is another testament of Jesus Christ and the great tool of conversion in the latter days. Our purpose in sharing the gospel is to invite all to come unto Jesus Christ,[3] receive the blessings of the restored gospel, and endure to the end through faith in the Savior.[4] Helping individuals to experience the mighty change of heart[5] and bind themselves to the Lord through sacred covenants and ordinances are the fundamental objectives of preaching the gospel.

Moroni's introduction of the Book of Mormon to Joseph Smith initiated the work of salvation and exaltation for individuals on *this side of the veil* in the dispensation of the fulness of times.

Continuing his instruction to Joseph, Moroni next quoted from the book of Malachi in the Old Testament, with a little variation in the language used in the King James version:

"Behold, I will reveal unto you the Priesthood, by the hand of

Elijah the prophet, before the coming of the great and dreadful day of the Lord.

". . . And he shall plant in the hearts of the children the promises made to the fathers, and the hearts of the children shall turn to their fathers. If it were not so, the whole earth would be utterly wasted at his coming."[6]

Our purpose in building temples is to make available the holy places wherein the sacred covenants and ordinances necessary for the salvation and exaltation of the human family can be administered, for both the living and the dead. Moroni's instruction to Joseph Smith about the vital role of Elijah and priesthood authority expanded the work of salvation and exaltation on *this side of the veil* and initiated in our dispensation the work for the dead on *the other side of the veil.*

In summary, Moroni's teachings in September of 1823 about the Book of Mormon and the mission of Elijah established the doctrinal foundation for the work of salvation and exaltation on *both sides of the veil.*

Teachings of the Prophet Joseph Smith

The lessons Joseph Smith learned from Moroni influenced every aspect of his ministry. For example, at a solemn assembly held in the Kirtland Temple on April 6, 1837, the Prophet declared, "After all that has been said, the greatest and most important duty is to preach the Gospel."[7]

Almost precisely seven years later, on April 7, 1844, Joseph Smith delivered a sermon known today as the King Follett Discourse. He declared in that address, "The greatest responsibility in this world that God has laid upon us is to seek after our dead."[8]

But how can preaching the gospel and seeking after our dead both be the single greatest duty and responsibility God has placed upon us? I believe the Prophet Joseph Smith was emphasizing in both statements the fundamental truth that covenants, entered into through authoritative priesthood ordinances, can bind us to the

Lord Jesus Christ and are the essential core of the work of salvation and exaltation on both sides of the veil.

Missionary and temple and family history work are complementary and interrelated aspects of one great work that focuses upon the sacred covenants and ordinances that enable us to receive the power of godliness in our lives and, ultimately, return to the presence of Heavenly Father. Thus, the two statements by the Prophet that initially may appear contradictory, in fact, highlight the focal point of this great latter-day work.

Bound to the Savior through Covenants and Ordinances

The Savior said:

"Take my yoke upon you, and learn of me; for I am meek and lowly in heart: and ye shall find rest unto your souls.

"For my yoke is easy, and my burden is light."[9]

We take the Savior's yoke upon us as we learn about, worthily receive, and honor sacred covenants and ordinances. We are bound securely to and with the Savior as we faithfully remember and do our best to live in accordance with the obligations we have accepted. And that bond with Him is the source of spiritual strength in every season of our lives.

The Covenant People of the Lord

I invite you to consider the blessings promised to covenant-keeping disciples of Jesus Christ. For example, Nephi "beheld the church of the Lamb of God [in the latter days], and its numbers were few, . . . the saints of God, were also upon all the face of the earth; and their dominions . . . were small."[10]

He also "beheld the power of the Lamb of God, that it descended upon the saints of the church of the Lamb, and *upon the covenant people of the Lord*, . . . and they were *armed with righteousness and with the power of God in great glory*."[11]

The phrase "armed with righteousness and with the power of God in great glory" is not simply a nice idea or an example of beautiful scriptural language. Rather, these blessings are readily evident in the lives of countless latter-day disciples of the Lord.

My assignments as a member of the Twelve take me all over the world. And I have been blessed to meet and learn memorable lessons from many of you. I testify that the covenant people of the Lord today indeed are armed with righteousness and with the power of God in great glory. I have witnessed faith, courage, perspective, persistence, and joy that extend far beyond mortal capacity—and that only God could provide.

I witnessed the righteousness and power of God in great glory, received through faithfulness to covenants and ordinances, in the life of a young Church member who was partially paralyzed in a horrific automobile accident. After this individual's grueling months of recovery and adapting to a new lifestyle with restricted mobility, I met and talked with this stalwart soul. During our conversation I asked, "What has this experience helped you to learn?" The immediate response was, "I am not sad. I am not mad. And everything will be OK."

I witnessed the righteousness and power of God in great glory, received through faithfulness to covenants and ordinances, in the lives of newly baptized and confirmed members of the Church. These converts were eager to learn and serve, willing but often unsure about how to set aside old habits and strong traditions, and yet joyful to become "fellowcitizens with the saints, and of the household of God."[12]

I witnessed the righteousness and power of God in great glory, received through faithfulness to covenants and ordinances, in the lives of a family who cared tenderly for a spouse and parent with a terminal disease. These valiant disciples described times that their family felt all alone—and times they knew the hand of the Lord was lifting and strengthening them. This family expressed sincere gratitude for the difficult mortal experiences that allow us to grow and become more like our Heavenly Father and our Redeemer, Jesus Christ. God succored and blessed this family with the companionship of the Holy Ghost and made their home as sacred a place of refuge as the temple.

I witnessed the righteousness and power of God in great glory, received through faithfulness to covenants and ordinances, in the life of a Church member who experienced the heartache of divorce. This sister's spiritual and emotional distress was heightened by a sense of unfairness associated with her spouse's violation of covenants and the breakup of their marriage. She wanted justice and accountability.

As this faithful woman was struggling with all that had happened to her, she studied and pondered the Savior's Atonement more intently and intensely than ever before in her life. Gradually, a deeper understanding of Christ's redemptive mission distilled upon her soul—His suffering for our sins and also for our pains, weaknesses, disappointments, and anguish. And she was inspired to ask herself a penetrating question: since the price already has been paid for those sins, would you demand that the price be paid twice? She realized that such a requirement would be neither just nor merciful.

This woman learned that binding herself to the Savior through covenants and ordinances can heal the wounds caused by another person's unrighteous exercise of moral agency and enabled her to find the capacity to forgive and receive peace, mercy, and love.

Promise and Testimony

Covenant promises and blessings are possible only because of our Savior, Jesus Christ. He invites us to look to Him,[13] come unto Him,[14] learn of Him,[15] and bind ourselves to Him[16] through the covenants and ordinances of His restored gospel. I testify and promise that honoring covenants arms us with righteousness and with the power of God in great glory. And I witness that the living Lord Jesus Christ is our Savior. Of these truths I joyfully testify in the sacred name of Jesus Christ, amen.

Notes

1. See Joseph Smith—History 1:29.
2. Joseph Smith—History 1:33.
3. See Moroni 10:30–33.
4. See *Preach My Gospel: A Guide to Missionary Service* (2019), 1.

5. See Alma 5:12–14.

6. Joseph Smith—History 1:38–39.

7. *Teachings of Presidents of the Church: Joseph Smith* (2007), 330; see also Joseph Smith discourse, 6 April 1837, in "Anniversary of the Church of Latter Day Saints," *Latter Day Saints' Messenger and Advocate* 3, no. 7 (April 1837), 487, josephsmithpapers.org/paper-summary/discourse-6-april-1837/1.

8. *Teachings: Joseph Smith*, 475; see also Joseph Smith discourse, 7 April 1844, in "Conference Minutes," *Times and Seasons* 5, no. 15 (August 15, 1844), 616, josephsmithpapers.org/paper-summary/minutes-and-discourses-6–7-april-1844-as-published-by-times-and-seasons/14.

9. Matthew 11:29–30.

10. 1 Nephi 14:12.

11. 1 Nephi 14:14; emphasis added.

12. Ephesians 2:19.

13. See Doctrine and Covenants 6:36.

14. See 3 Nephi 12:20; Moroni 10:32–33.

15. See Matthew 11:29; Doctrine and Covenants 19:23.

16. See Doctrine and Covenants 43:9; 82:10.

FAITH TO ACT AND BECOME

ELDER CIRO SCHMEIL
Of the Seventy

Shortly after I was called to serve as a General Authority Seventy, I had the opportunity to visit with President Russell M. Nelson for a few minutes. It was an unplanned encounter in the cafeteria, and he was so kind to invite Elder S. Mark Palmer and me to sit and enjoy lunch with him.

"What do we talk about during lunch with the prophet?" was the thought that came to my mind. So I decided to ask President Nelson if he had any counsel or guidance for me since I was just starting my calling. His answer was very simple and direct; he looked at me and said, "Elder Schmeil, you are called for what you can become." I walked away from that experience pondering about what the Lord wants me to become. As I thought about this, I realized that He wants me to become a better husband, father, and son and a better servant. I then realized that all of this could be accomplished as I worked to become a better disciple of the Savior Jesus Christ.

Last general conference, President Nelson said: "To do anything well requires effort. Becoming a true disciple of Jesus Christ is no exception."[1] President Nelson is inviting us to work hard to become better disciples of Jesus Christ. He told us that to become more like the Savior, we need to strengthen our faith by asking, acting, and studying, among other things.

1. Ask

He said, "Ask your Heavenly Father, in the name of Jesus Christ, for help."[2] Asking through prayer is one of the keys to knowing how to become a better disciple of Jesus Christ.

Toward the end of His ministry among the Nephites in the Americas, Jesus Christ ascended into heaven. Later, His disciples gathered together, "united in mighty prayer and fasting. And Jesus again showed himself unto them, for they were praying unto the

Father in his name."[3] Why did Jesus show Himself again to His disciples? Because they were praying; they were asking.

Then He continued:

"Now I go unto the Father. And verily I say unto you, whatsoever things ye shall ask the Father in my name shall be given unto you.

"Therefore, ask, and ye shall receive; knock, and it shall be opened unto you; for he that asketh, receiveth; and unto him that knocketh, it shall be opened."[4]

We need to ask in faith to know the will of the Lord and accept that the Lord knows what is better for us.

2. Act

Acting is another essential key to becoming a better disciple of Jesus Christ. As we act, He will guide and direct us along the way. I am sure that Nephi was seeking guidance from the Lord to know how to get the brass plates from Laban, yet he and his brothers tried twice without success. But they were acting, and the Lord was directing them along the way. Finally, Nephi was successful the third time. He recalled, "I was led by the Spirit, not knowing beforehand the things which I should do."[5]

This is how the Lord works as we put forth effort and act, even when we do not have a clear understanding of what needs to be done. The Lord told Nephi *what* to do: go and get the plates. But He did not tell Nephi *how* to do it. He left it to Nephi to figure out and seek the Lord's help—and this is often how the Lord works in our lives. As we act in faith, the Lord guides and directs us.

3. Study

In 3 Nephi, the disciples mentioned to the Savior that there were disputations among the people regarding the name of the Church. In response, the Savior taught an important principle when He asked, "Have they not read the scriptures?"[6] Studying is then another essential key to becoming a better disciple of Jesus Christ. Prayer and scripture study go hand in hand. They work together for our benefit. This is the process that the Lord has established. "Feast upon the words of Christ; for behold, the words of Christ will tell you all things what ye should do."[7]

The Savior also taught that we should not only study the scriptures but also teach from them, as He demonstrated to the Nephites: "And now it came to pass that when Jesus had expounded all the scriptures in one, which they had written, he commanded them that they should teach the things which he had expounded unto them."[8]

This is one of the reasons why it was so important for Nephi to go back and get the brass plates: his family needed the scriptures not only to help them journey to the promised land but also to help them teach their children. We too must seek guidance from the scriptures for our journey, and we must teach from them in our homes and Church callings.

4. Act to Become

Many times answers to prayer will not come right away. But we must have faith to continue, act in righteousness, and be persistent like Nephi when he was trying to get the brass plates. The Lord will show us a little bit at a time; as we study the scriptures, the Lord will give us the answers or the necessary strength for us to get through one more day, one more week, and to try one more time. Elder Richard G. Scott said: "Be thankful that sometimes God lets you struggle for a long time before that answer comes. That causes your faith to increase and your character to grow."[9]

Through prayer and scripture study, the Lord has always given me the strength to act and endure one more day, one more week, and to try one more time. Many times the answers did not come right away. I have questions that have not been answered yet, but I keep asking and studying, and I am happy that the Lord continues to give me the strength to act as I wait for answers.

Elder Scott also said, "As you walk to the boundary of your understanding into the twilight of uncertainty, exercising faith, you will be led to find solutions you would not obtain otherwise."[10]

To become a better follower of the Savior Jesus Christ is a

lifelong journey, and we are all in different stages, moving at a different pace. We must keep in mind that this is not a competition, and we are here to love and help each other. We need to be acting in order to allow the Savior to work with us in our lives.

Speaking to Sidney Rigdon, the Lord said the following: "I have looked upon thee and thy works. I have heard thy prayers, and prepared thee for a greater work."[11] I testify that the Lord hears and answers our prayers; He knows us; He has a great work for each one of us. Through prayer, scripture study, and action, we can unlock the blessings of heaven and become better followers of the Savior Jesus Christ.

President Dallin H. Oaks taught that "the Final Judgment is not just an evaluation of a sum total of good and evil acts—what we have *done*. It is an acknowledgment of the final effect of our acts and thoughts—what we have *become*."[12]

I am grateful for prophets, seers, and revelators; they are the watchmen on the tower. They see things that we do not see. I testify that through their words, we can become better followers of the Savior Jesus Christ and achieve our potential. I testify that Christ lives and knows each one of us individually. This is His Church. In the sacred name of Jesus Christ, amen.

Notes

1. Russell M. Nelson, "Christ Is Risen; Faith in Him Will Move Mountains," *Liahona*, May 2021, 103.
2. Russell M. Nelson, "Christ Is Risen; Faith in Him Will Move Mountains," 103.
3. 3 Nephi 27:1–2.
4. 3 Nephi 27:28–29.
5. 1 Nephi 4:6.
6. 3 Nephi 27:5.
7. 2 Nephi 32:3.
8. 3 Nephi 23:14.
9. Richard G. Scott, "The Transforming Power of Faith and Character," *Ensign* or *Liahona*, Nov. 2010, 44.
10. Richard G. Scott, "The Transforming Power of Faith and Character," 44.
11. Doctrine and Covenants 35:3.
12. Dallin H. Oaks, "The Challenge to Become," *Ensign*, Nov. 2000, 32; *Liahona*, Jan. 2001, 40.

GOD'S LOVE: THE MOST JOYOUS TO THE SOUL

SUSAN H. PORTER

First Counselor in the Primary General Presidency

Brothers and sisters, do you know how completely God, our Heavenly Father, loves you? Have you felt His love deep in your soul?

When you know and understand how completely you are loved as a child of God, it changes everything. It changes the way you feel about yourself when you make mistakes. It changes how you feel when difficult things happen. It changes your view of God's commandments. It changes your view of others and of your capacity to make a difference.

Elder Jeffrey R. Holland taught: "The first great *commandment* of all eternity is to love God with all of *our* heart, might, mind, and strength—that's the first great commandment. But the first great *truth* of all eternity is that God loves *us* with all of *His* heart, might, mind, and strength."[1]

How can each of us know deep in our souls that great truth of eternity?

The prophet Nephi was shown in a vision the most powerful evidence of God's love. Upon viewing the tree of life, Nephi asked to know the interpretation thereof. In answer, an angel showed Nephi a city, a mother, and a baby. As Nephi looked upon the city of Nazareth and the righteous mother Mary, holding the infant Jesus in her arms, the angel declared, "Behold the Lamb of God, yea, even the Son of the Eternal Father!"[2]

At that sacred moment, Nephi understood that in the birth of the Savior, God was showing forth His pure and complete love. God's love, Nephi testified, "*sheddeth itself abroad* in the hearts of the children of men."[3]

We can picture the love of God as light emanating from the tree of life, shedding itself abroad over all the earth into the hearts of the children of men. God's light and love permeate all His creations.[4]

Sometimes we mistakenly think that we can feel God's love only *after* we have followed the iron rod and partaken of the fruit. God's love, however, not only is received by those who come *to* the tree but is the very power that motivates us to *seek* that tree.

"Wherefore, it is the most desirable above all things," Nephi taught, and the angel exclaimed, "Yea, and the most joyous to the soul."[5]

Twenty years ago, a beloved family member stepped away from the Church. He had many unanswered questions. His wife, a convert, stayed true to her faith. They worked hard to preserve their marriage in the differences that arose.

Last year he wrote down three questions about the Church that were difficult for him to reconcile and sent them to two couples who had been his friends for several years. He invited them to reflect on those questions and come to dinner to share their thoughts.

Following this visit with friends, he went to his room and started working on a project. The evening conversation and the love shown to him by his friends came to the forefront of his mind. He later wrote that he was compelled to stop his work. He said: "A bright light filled my soul. . . . I was familiar with this deep feeling of enlightenment, but in this case it continued to grow stronger than ever before and lasted for several minutes. I sat quietly with the feeling, which I came to understand as a manifestation of the love of God for me. . . . I felt a spiritual impression that told me I could return to church and express this love of God in what I do there."

He then wondered about his questions. The feeling he received was that God honored his questions and that not having clear answers should not stop him from moving forward.[6] He should share God's love with all while he continued to contemplate. As he acted on that impression, he felt a kinship with Joseph Smith, who remarked after his First Vision, "My soul was filled with love, and for many days I could rejoice with great joy."[7]

Remarkably, a few short months later, this family member received the same calling he had held 20 years before. The first time he held the calling, he performed his responsibilities as a dutiful member of the Church. Now the question for him became not "How can I fulfill this calling?" but "How can I show God's love through my service?" With this new approach, he felt joy, meaning, and purpose in all aspects of his calling.

Sisters and brothers, how can we receive the transforming power of God's love? The prophet Mormon invites us to "pray unto the Father with all the energy of heart, that ye may be filled with this love, which he hath bestowed upon all who are true followers of his Son, Jesus Christ."[8] Mormon is inviting us not only to pray that we may be filled with His love for *others* but to pray that we may know of God's pure love for *ourselves.*[9]

As we receive His love, we find greater joy in striving to love and serve as He did, becoming "true followers of his Son, Jesus Christ."[10]

God's love is not found in the *circumstances* of our lives but in His *presence* in our lives. We know of His love when we receive strength beyond our own and when His Spirit brings peace, comfort, and direction. At times it may be difficult to feel His love. We can pray to have our eyes opened to see His hand in our lives and to see His love in the beauty of His creations.

As we ponder the Savior's life and His infinite sacrifice, we begin to understand His love for us. We reverently sing the words of Eliza R. Snow: "His precious blood he freely spilt; His life he freely gave."[11] Jesus's humility in suffering for us distills upon our souls, opening our hearts to seek forgiveness at His hand and filling us with a desire to live as He did.[12]

President Russell M. Nelson wrote, "The more committed we become to patterning our lives after His, the purer and more divine our love becomes."[13]

Our son related: "When I was 11, my friends and I decided to hide from our teacher and skip the first half of our Primary class. When we finally arrived, to our surprise, the teacher greeted us warmly. He then offered a heartfelt prayer during which he expressed sincere gratitude to the Lord that we had decided to come to class that day *of our own free will.* I cannot remember what the lesson was about or even our teacher's name, but now, some 30 years later, I am still touched by the pure love he showed me that day."

Five years ago, I observed an example of divine love while attending Primary in Russia. I saw a faithful sister kneel in front of two children and testify to them that even if they were the only ones living on earth, Jesus would have suffered and died just for them.

I testify that our Lord and Savior did indeed die for each and every one of us. It was an expression of His infinite love for us and for His Father.

"I know that my Redeemer lives. What comfort this sweet sentence gives! . . . He lives to bless [us] with his love."[14]

May we open our hearts to receive the pure love that God has for us and then shed forth His love in all we do and are. In the sacred name of Jesus Christ, amen.

Notes

1. Jeffrey R. Holland, "Tomorrow the Lord Will Do Wonders among You," *Ensign* or *Liahona*, May 2016, 127.
2. 1 Nephi 11:21.
3. 1 Nephi 11:22; emphasis added.
4. See Doctrine and Covenants 88:13.
5. 1 Nephi 11:22, 23.
6. See 1 Nephi 11:17.
7. Joseph Smith, in Karen Lynn Davidson and others, eds., *The Joseph Smith Papers, Histories, Volume 1: Joseph Smith Histories, 1832–1844* (2012), 13; punctuation and capitalization modernized.
8. Moroni 7:48.
9. See Neill F. Marriott, "Abiding in God and Repairing the Breach," *Ensign* or *Liahona*, Nov. 2017, 11: "Perhaps our life in a loving premortal world set up our yearning for true, lasting love here on earth. We are divinely designed to give love and be loved, and the deepest love comes when we are one with God."
10. Moroni 7:48.
11. "How Great the Wisdom and the Love," *Hymns*, no. 195.
12. See Linda S. Reeves, "Worthy of Our Promised Blessings," *Ensign* or *Liahona*, Nov. 2015, 11: "I believe that if we could daily remember and recognize the depth of that love our Heavenly Father and our Savior have for us, we would be willing to do anything to be back in Their presence again, surrounded by Their love eternally."
13. Russell M. Nelson, "Divine Love," *Ensign*, Feb. 2003, 25; *Liahona*, Feb. 2003, 17.
14. "I Know That My Redeemer Lives," *Hymns*, no. 136.

ADDRESSING MENTAL HEALTH

ELDER ERICH W. KOPISCHKE
Of the Seventy

Even though our family has enjoyed rich blessings while joyfully walking the covenant path, we have also faced exceedingly high mountains. I wish to share some very personal experiences regarding mental illness. These include clinical depression, severe anxiety, bipolar disorder, ADHD—and sometimes a combination of them all. I share these tender experiences with the approval of those involved.

During my ministry, I have encountered hundreds of individuals and families with similar experiences. Sometimes I wonder if the "desolating sickness" covering the land, as mentioned in the scriptures, might include mental illness.[1] It is worldwide, covering every continent and culture, and affecting all—young, old, rich, and poor. Members of the Church have not been excluded.

At the same time, our doctrine teaches us to strive to become like Jesus Christ and be perfected in Him. Our children sing, "I'm trying to be like Jesus."[2] We long to be perfect even as our Heavenly Father and Jesus Christ are perfect.[3] Because mental illness can interfere with our perception of perfection, it remains all too often a taboo. As a result, there is too much ignorance, too much silent suffering, and too much despair. Many, feeling overwhelmed because they do not meet perceived standards, mistakenly believe they have no place in the Church.

To combat such deception, it is important to remember that "the Savior loves each of His Father's children. He fully comprehends the pain and struggle that many experience as they live with a broad range of mental health challenges. He suffered 'pains and afflictions and temptations of *every* kind; . . . [taking] upon him the pains and the sicknesses of his people' (Alma 7:11; emphasis added; see also Hebrews 4:15–16; 2 Nephi 9:21). Because He understands all afflictions, He knows how 'to heal the brokenhearted' (Luke 4:18; see also Isaiah 49:13–16)."[4] Challenges often indicate a need for additional tools and support and are not a character defect.

Allow me to share several observations I made as our family has passed through trials.

First, many people will mourn with us; they won't judge us. Due to severe panic attacks, anxiety, and depression, our son returned home from his mission after just four weeks. As his parents, we found it difficult to deal with disappointment and sadness because we had prayed so much for his success. Like all parents, we want our children to prosper and be happy. A mission was to be an important milestone for our son. We also wondered what other people might think.

Unbeknownst to us, our son's return was infinitely more devastating for him. Note that he loved the Lord and wanted to serve, and yet he could not for reasons he struggled to understand. He soon found himself at a point of total hopelessness, battling deep guilt. He no longer felt accepted but spiritually numb. He became consumed by recurring thoughts of death.

While in this irrational state, our son believed that the only action left was to take his own life. It took the Holy Ghost and a legion of angels on both sides of the veil to save him.

While he was fighting for his life and during this immensely difficult time, our family, ward leaders, members, and friends went out of their way to support and minister to us.

I have never felt such an outpouring of love. I have never sensed more powerfully and in such a personal way what it means to comfort those in need of comfort. Our family will be ever grateful for that outpouring.

I cannot describe the countless miracles that accompanied these events. Gratefully, our son survived, but it has taken a long time and much medical, therapeutic, and spiritual care for him to heal and to accept that he is loved, valued, and needed.

I recognize that not all such incidents end like ours. I sorrow with those who have lost loved ones far too early and are now left with feelings of grief as well as unanswered questions.

My next observation is that it can be difficult for parents to identify their children's struggles, but we must educate ourselves.

How can we know the difference between the difficulties associated with normal development and signs of illness? As parents, we have the sacred charge to help our children navigate life's challenges; however, few of us are mental health specialists. We nevertheless need to care for our children by helping them learn to be content with their sincere efforts as they strive to meet appropriate expectations. Each of us knows from our own personal shortcomings that spiritual growth is an ongoing process.

We now understand that "there is not a simple cure-all for emotional and mental wellness. We will experience stress and turmoil because we live in a fallen world with a fallen body. Additionally, many contributing factors may lead to a diagnosis of mental illness. Regardless of our mental and emotional well-being, focusing on growth is healthier than obsessing about our shortcomings."[5]

For my wife and me, the one thing that has always helped us was staying as close to the Lord as possible. In hindsight, we now see how the Lord patiently tutored us through times of great uncertainty. His light guided us step by step through the darkest hours. The Lord helped us to see that the worth of an individual soul is far more important in the eternal scheme than any earthly task or achievement.

Again, educating ourselves about mental illness prepares us to help ourselves and others who might be struggling. Open and honest discussion with one another will help this important topic to receive the attention it deserves. After all, information precedes inspiration and revelation. These all-too-often invisible challenges can affect anyone, and when we are facing them, they appear insurmountable.

One of the first things we need to learn is that we are certainly not alone. I invite you to study the topic of mental health in the Life Help section of the Gospel Library app. Learning will lead to more understanding, more acceptance, more compassion, more love. It can lessen tragedy while helping us develop and manage healthy expectations and healthy interactions.

My final observation: we need to constantly watch over each other. We must love one another and be less judgmental—especially when our expectations are not immediately met. We should help our children and youth feel the love of Jesus Christ in their lives, even when they struggle to personally feel love for themselves. Elder Orson F. Whitney, who served as a member of the Quorum of the Twelve Apostles, counseled parents how to help struggling offspring: "Pray for your . . . children; hold on to them with your faith."[6]

I have often pondered what it means to hold on to them with faith. I believe it includes simple acts of love, meekness, kindness, and respect. It means allowing them to develop at their own pace and bearing testimony to help them feel our Savior's love. It requires us to think more about them and less about ourselves or others. That usually means speaking less and listening much, much more. We must love them, empower them, and praise them often in their efforts to succeed and be faithful to God. And finally, we should do everything in our power to stay close to them—just as we stay close to God.

For all who are personally affected by mental illness, hold fast to your covenants, even if you might not feel God's love at this time. Do whatever lies in your power and then "stand still . . . to see the salvation of God, and for his arm to be revealed."[7]

I testify that Jesus Christ is our Savior. He knows us. He loves us, and He will wait on us. During our family's trials, I have come to know just how close He is. His promises are true:

> *Fear not, I am with thee; oh, be not dismayed,*
> *For I am thy God and will still give thee aid.*
> *I'll strengthen thee, help thee, and cause thee to stand, . . .*
> *Upheld by my righteous, omnipotent hand.*

Knowing how firm our foundation is, may we ever joyfully declare:

> *The soul that on Jesus hath leaned for repose*
> *I will not, I cannot, desert to his foes;*
> *That soul, though all hell should endeavor to shake, . . .*
> *I'll never, no never, no never forsake!*[8]

In the name of Jesus Christ, amen.

Notes

1. Doctrine and Covenants 45:31.
2. "I'm Trying to Be like Jesus," *Children's Songbook*, 78–79.
3. See 3 Nephi 12:48.
4. "Like a Broken Vessel," Mental Health: General Principles, ChurchofJesusChrist.org.
5. Sheldon Martin, "Strive to Be—a Pattern for Growth and Mental and Emotional Wellness," *Liahona*, Aug. 2021, 14.
6. Orson F. Whitney, in Conference Report, Apr. 1929, 110.
7. Doctrine and Covenants 123:17.
8. "How Firm a Foundation," *Hymns*, no. 85.

THE THINGS OF MY SOUL

ELDER RONALD A. RASBAND
Of the Quorum of the Twelve Apostles

My brothers and sisters, as I stand in our beloved Conference Center once again, I am reminded of the words of the Apostle Peter: "Lord, it is good for us to be here."[1]

My thoughts today are centered on the words of the prophet Nephi, who kept the record of his people following Father Lehi's death. Nephi wrote, "And upon these I write the things of my soul."[2]

I used to pass over this verse, thinking the word *things* was not very elegant or spiritual, not grand enough to pair with "my soul." Yet I have learned that the word *things* is used in the scriptures 2,354 times.[3] For example, in Moses: "I am the Beginning and the End, the Almighty God; by mine Only Begotten I created these *things*."[4] And Nephi's words: "Behold, my soul delighteth in the *things* of the Lord; and my heart pondereth continually upon the *things* which I have seen and heard."[5]

Nephi's words raise the questions "What things do you ponder?" "What things really matter to you?" "What are the things of your soul?"

The things of our souls are often clarified and deepened by asking questions.

During the pandemic I have met with youth from all over the world in many devotionals, large and small, through broadcasts and social media, and we have discussed their questions.

Fourteen-year-old Joseph Smith had a question deep in his soul, and he took it to the Lord. President Russell M. Nelson has emphasized: "Take your questions to the Lord and to other faithful sources. Study with the desire to *believe* rather than with the hope that you can find a flaw in the fabric of a prophet's life or a discrepancy in the scriptures. Stop increasing your doubts by rehearsing them with . . . doubters. Allow the Lord to lead you on your journey of spiritual discovery."[6]

Youth often ask me what I believe and why I believe.

I remember visiting virtually with one young woman in her home. I asked if it was the first time an Apostle had been in her home. She quickly smiled and responded, "Yes." Her question for me was good: "What are the most important *things* I should know?"

I answered with the things of my soul, the things that prepare me to hear promptings, that lift my sights beyond the ways of the world, that give purpose to my work in the gospel and to my very life.

May I share with you some of the things of my soul? These things apply to all who seek to be true disciples of Jesus Christ. Ten would be a good, round number. Today I am giving you seven with the hope that you will complete eight, nine, and ten from your own experiences.

First, love God the Father and Jesus Christ, our Savior.

Jesus decreed the first great commandment: "Thou shalt love the Lord thy God with all thy heart, and with all thy soul, and with all thy mind."[7]

President Nelson declared his devotion to God, our Eternal Father, and to His Son, Jesus Christ, when he was called to lead the Lord's Church, saying, "I know Them, love Them, and pledge to serve Them—and you—with every remaining breath of my life."[8]

So first, love the Father and the Son.

Second, "Love thy neighbour."[9]

That is not just a good idea; it's the second great commandment. Your neighbors are your spouse and family, ward members, work colleagues, roommates, those not of our faith, those needing a helping hand, and, frankly, everyone. The essence of "love thy neighbour" is voiced in the hymn "Love One Another."[10]

President Nelson reminds us, "When we love *God* with all our hearts, He turns our hearts to the well-being of *others*."[11]

Third, love yourself.

This is where many struggle. Isn't it curious that loving ourselves seems to come less easily than loving others? Yet the Lord has said, "Love thy neighbour as thyself."[12] He values the divinity within us, and so must we. When we are heavy laden with mistakes, heartaches, feelings of inadequacy, disappointment, anger, or sin, the power of the Savior's Atonement is, by divine design, one of the things that lifts the soul.

Fourth, keep the commandments.

The Lord has made it clear: "If ye love me, keep my commandments."[13] Strive each day to be and do a little better and to press forward in righteousness.

Fifth, always be worthy to attend the temple.

I call it being recommended to the Lord. Whether you have access to a temple or not, being worthy of a current temple recommend keeps you firmly focused on the things that matter, the covenant path.

Sixth, be joyful and cheerful.

"Be of good cheer, and do not fear,"[14] the Lord has said. Why? How, when challenges face us at every turn? Because of the promise made by Jesus Christ: "I the Lord am with you, and will stand by you."[15]

President Nelson describes the restored gospel as "a message of *joy*!"[16] And he explains, "The joy we feel has little to do with the circumstances of our lives and everything to do with the focus of our lives."[17]

Seventh, follow God's living prophet.

This may be seventh on my list of things, but it is at the top of my mind in terms of its importance today.

We have a prophet of God on the earth today! Never discount what that means for you. Remember the young woman I mentioned at the beginning. She wanted to know what things matter most. "Follow the living prophet," I said then and I emphasize again today.

We are distinguished as a Church to be led by prophets, seers, and revelators called of God for this time. I promise that as you listen and follow their counsel, you will never be led astray. Never!

We live in a time when we are "tossed to and fro,"[18] when spirituality, decency, integrity, and respect are under attack. We have to make choices. We have the voice of the Lord through His prophet to calm our fears and lift our sights, for when President Nelson speaks, he speaks for the Lord.

We are blessed with scriptures and teachings that remind us, "My thoughts are not your thoughts, neither are your ways my ways, saith the Lord."[19]

So it was with Naaman, a great military leader in Syria, yet a leper, who was told that the prophet Elisha could heal him. Elisha sent his messenger to tell Naaman to wash in the River Jordan seven times and he would be clean. Naaman scoffed. Certainly there was a mightier river than the Jordan, and why send a servant when he expected Elisha, the prophet, to personally heal him? Naaman walked away but eventually was persuaded by his servants: "If the prophet had bid thee do some great thing, wouldest thou not have done it?"[20] Naaman finally dipped seven times in the Jordan and was healed.

The account of Naaman reminds us of the risk of picking and choosing the parts of prophetic counsel that fit our thinking, our expectations, or today's norms. Our prophet continually points us to our own River Jordans to be healed.

The most important words we can hear, ponder, and follow are those revealed through our living prophet. I bear witness that I have sat in counsel with President Nelson to discuss weighty matters of the Church and of the world, and I have seen revelation flow through him. He knows the Lord, he knows His ways, and he desires that all of God's children will hear Him, the Lord Jesus Christ.

For many years we heard from the prophet twice a year at general conference. But with the complex issues of our day, President Nelson is speaking much more often in forums,[21] social media,[22] devotionals,[23] and even press briefings.[24] I have observed him preparing and presenting profound revelatory messages that have encouraged more gratitude, promoted greater inclusion of all our brothers and sisters on earth, and increased peace, hope, joy, health, and healing in our individual lives.

President Nelson is a gifted communicator, but more important, he is a prophet of God. That is staggering when you think about it, but it is critical to realize that his clear direction will shield us all from the deceit, craftiness, and secular ways gaining momentum in the world today.[25]

The prophetic mantle is all about revelation. "The Restoration of the Fulness of the Gospel of Jesus Christ: A Bicentennial Proclamation to the World," given in the April 2020 general conference, emphasizes that the Lord is directing this work. In this proclamation, the First Presidency and Quorum of the Twelve Apostles state: "We gladly declare that the promised Restoration goes forward through continuing revelation. The earth will never again be the same, as God will 'gather together in one all things in Christ' (Ephesians 1:10)."[26]

"All things in Christ"[27] and "the things of my soul"[28] are what this Church, this gospel, and this people are all about.

I close with an invitation for each of you to consider the seven "things of my soul" I have shared today: love God the Father and Jesus Christ, our Savior; love your neighbor; love yourself; keep the commandments; always be worthy of a temple recommend; be joyful and cheerful; and follow God's living prophet. I invite you to identify your own eight, nine, and ten. Consider ways you might share your heartfelt "things" with others and encourage them to pray, ponder, and seek the Lord's guidance.

The things of my soul are as precious to me as yours are to you. These things strengthen our service in the Church and in all areas of life. They commit us to Jesus Christ, they remind us of our covenants, and they help us feel secure in the arms of the Lord. I testify that He desires that our souls "shall never hunger nor thirst, but shall be filled"[29] with His love as we seek to become His true disciples, to be one with Him as He is with the Father. In the name of Jesus Christ, amen.

Notes

1. Matthew 17:4.
2. 2 Nephi 4:15.
3. See Scripture Citation Index, scriptures.byu.edu.
4. Moses 2:1; emphasis added.
5. 2 Nephi 4:16; emphasis added.
6. Russell M. Nelson, "Christ Is Risen; Faith in Him Will Move Mountains," *Liahona*, May 2021, 103.

7. Matthew 22:37.
8. Russell M. Nelson, "As We Go Forward Together," *Ensign* or *Liahona*, Apr. 2018, 7.
9. Matthew 22:39.
10. "Love One Another," *Hymns*, no. 308.
11. Russell M. Nelson, "The Second Great Commandment," *Ensign* or *Liahona*, Nov. 2019, 97.
12. Matthew 22:39.
13. John 14:15.
14. Doctrine and Covenants 68:6.
15. Doctrine and Covenants 68:6.
16. Russell M. Nelson, "Welcome Message," *Liahona*, May 2021, 7.
17. Russell M. Nelson, "Joy and Spiritual Survival," *Ensign* or *Liahona*, Nov. 2016, 82.
18. Ephesians 4:14.
19. Isaiah 55:8.
20. 2 Kings 5:13.
21. For example, see Friend to Friend Broadcast for Children: 2021 (Feb. 20, 2021), broadcasts .ChurchofJesusChrist.org, part 3, from time code 9:57 to 13:16.
22. For examples, see Russell M. Nelson, Facebook, July 23, 2021, facebook.com/russell.m.nelson; "President Russell M. Nelson on the Healing Power of Gratitude" (video), ChurchofJesusChrist .org; Russell M. Nelson, Twitter, May 6, 2021, twitter.com/NelsonRussellM.
23. For example, see Russell M. Nelson, "The Love and Laws of God" (Brigham Young University devotional, Sept. 17, 2019), speeches.byu.edu.
24. For example, see "First Presidency and NAACP Leaders Announce a Shared Vision to 'Learn from and Serve One Another'" (news release, June 14, 2021), newsroom.ChurchofJesusChrist .org.
25. See Ephesians 4:11–14.
26. "The Restoration of the Fulness of the Gospel of Jesus Christ: A Bicentennial Proclamation to the World," ChurchofJesusChrist.org.
27. Ephesians 1:10.
28. 2 Nephi 4:15.
29. 3 Nephi 20:8.

PREPARING FOR THE SECOND COMING OF CHRIST

ELDER CHRISTOFFEL GOLDEN

Of the Seventy

As recorded in the Book of Mormon, six years before the birth of Jesus Christ, Samuel, a righteous Lamanite, prophesied to a Nephite people, who by then had become mostly apostate,[1] of the signs that would accompany our Savior's birth. Tragically, most Nephites rejected those signs because it was "not reasonable that such a being as a Christ [should] come."[2]

Regrettably, according to the scriptural record, many of the Jews, in like manner, could not accept that a man named Jesus, from the little-regarded province of Galilee, was indeed the long-awaited Messiah.[3] Jesus, who had indeed come to fulfill the many prophecies made by Hebrew prophets, was rejected and even crucified because, as the Book of Mormon prophet Jacob taught, the Jews were "looking beyond the mark." Consequently, Jacob testified that "God hath taken away his plainness from them, and delivered unto them many things which they cannot understand, because they desired it. And because they desired it God hath done it, that they may stumble."[4]

Strange as it may seem, no teaching, no miracle, and no appearance even of a heavenly angel, as witnessed by Laman and Lemuel,[5] appears to have the persuasive power to convince some individuals to alter their course, outlook, or belief that something is true. This is especially the case when teachings or miracles do not agree with an individual's preconceived whims, wishes, or ideas.

Please contrast for a moment the following two scriptures, the first from the Apostle Paul speaking of the latter days, describing the ways of man, and the second from Alma the prophet showing how God does His work among mankind. First from Paul:

"This know also, that in the last days perilous times shall come.

"For men shall be lovers of their own selves, covetous, boasters, proud, blasphemers, disobedient to parents, unthankful, unholy,

"Without natural affection, trucebreakers, false accusers, incontinent, fierce, despisers of those that are good,

"Traitors, heady, highminded, lovers of pleasures more than lovers of God; . . .

"Ever learning, and never able to come to the knowledge of the truth."[6]

And now from Alma, stating a foundational principle of the gospel of Jesus Christ: "Now ye may suppose that this is foolishness in me; but behold I say unto you, that by small and simple things are great things brought to pass; and small means in many instances doth confound the wise."[7]

We live in a modern world filled with great knowledge and much prowess. Nonetheless, these things too often camouflage the unsteady foundation upon which they are built. Consequently, they do not lead to real truth and on toward God and the power to receive revelation, acquire spiritual knowledge, and develop faith in Jesus Christ that leads to salvation.[8]

We are profoundly reminded of our Lord's words to Thomas and the other Apostles on the eve of His atoning sacrifice: "Jesus saith unto him, I am the way, the truth, and the life: no man cometh unto the Father, but by me."[9]

For those who have eyes to see, ears to hear, and hearts to feel, more than ever before we are required to confront the reality that we are getting ever closer to the Second Coming of Jesus Christ. True, great difficulties yet await those on the earth at His return, but in this regard, the faithful need not fear.

Now I quote for a moment from the Church's Gospel Topics under the heading "Second Coming of Jesus Christ":

"When the Savior comes again, He will come in power and glory to claim the earth as His kingdom. His Second Coming will mark the beginning of the Millennium.

"The Second Coming will be a fearful, mournful time for the wicked, but it will be a day of peace for the righteous. The Lord declared:

"'They that are wise and have received the truth, and have taken the Holy Spirit for their guide, and have not been deceived—verily I say unto you, they shall not be hewn down and cast into the fire, but shall abide the day.

"'And the earth shall be given unto them for an inheritance; and they shall multiply and wax strong, and their children shall grow up without sin unto salvation.

"'For the Lord shall be in their midst, and his glory shall be upon them, and he will be their king and their lawgiver' (Doctrine and Covenants 45:57–59)."[10]

In our preparation for the Second Coming of Jesus Christ, I provide a vital, comforting note for the faithful taken from the Old Testament prophet Amos: "Surely the Lord God will do nothing, until he revealeth his secret unto his servants the prophets."[11]

In this spirit, today's prophet of the Lord to the world, President Russell M. Nelson, has given us this recent inspiring counsel: "The gospel of Jesus Christ *is* a gospel of repentance. Because of the Savior's Atonement, His gospel provides an invitation to keep changing, growing, and becoming more pure. It is a gospel of hope, of healing, and of progress. Thus, the gospel is a message of *joy*! Our spirits rejoice with every small step forward we take."[12]

I unreservedly testify of and attest to the reality of God and the miracles in the everyday life of countless people from both the low and high stations of life. True, many sacred experiences are rarely spoken of, in part because of their divine origin and the resulting possibility of ridicule by some who do not know better.

In this regard, the last of the Book of Mormon prophets, Moroni, reminds us:

"And again I speak unto you who deny the revelations of God, and say that they are done away, that there are no revelations, nor prophecies, nor gifts, nor healing, nor speaking with tongues, and the interpretation of tongues;

"Behold I say unto you, he that denieth these things knoweth not the gospel of Christ; yea, he has not read the scriptures; if so, he does not understand them.

"For do we not read that God is the same yesterday, today,

and forever, and in him there is no variableness neither shadow of changing?"[13]

I conclude my remarks with a truly inspiring prophetic declaration from the Prophet Joseph Smith, given near the end of his ministry as he looked forward to the Second Coming of Jesus Christ: "Shall we not go on in so great a cause? Go forward and not backward. Courage, brethren [and, may I add, sisters]; and on, on to the victory! Let your hearts rejoice, and be exceedingly glad."[14] To which I add my witness in the name of Jesus Christ, amen.

Notes

1. See Helaman 13:12.
2. Helaman 16:18.
3. See John 7:47–52.
4. Jacob 4:14.
5. See 1 Nephi 3:29–31.
6. 2 Timothy 3:1–4, 7.
7. Alma 37:6.
8. See Helaman 5:12.
9. John 14:6.
10. Gospel Topics, "Second Coming of Jesus Christ," topics.ChurchofJesusChrist.org.
11. Joseph Smith Translation, Amos 3:7 (in Amos 3:7, footnote *a*).
12. Russell M. Nelson, "Welcome Message," *Liahona*, May 2021, 7.
13. Mormon 9:7–9.
14. Doctrine and Covenants 128:22.

FAVORED OF THE LORD IN ALL MY DAYS

ELDER MOISÉS VILLANUEVA
Of the Seventy

The COVID-19 pandemic has been one of the many trials and challenges that God's children have confronted throughout the history of the world. At the beginning of this year, my beloved family and I lived through some dark days. The pandemic and other causes brought death and pain to our family through the passing of some dear loved ones. Despite medical attention, fasting, and prayer, during the course of five weeks my brother Charly, my sister Susy, and my brother-in-law Jimmy crossed to the other side of the veil.

At times I have wondered why the Savior cried when He saw Mary anguished by the death of her brother, Lazarus, even though He knew that He had the power to raise Lazarus and that very soon He would use this power to rescue His friend from death.[1] I am amazed by the Savior's compassion and empathy for Mary; He understood the indescribable pain that Mary felt at the death of her brother, Lazarus.

We feel that same intense pain when we experience the temporary separation from our loved ones. The Savior has perfect compassion for us. He doesn't fault us for our shortsightedness nor for being limited in visualizing our eternal journey. Rather, He has compassion for our sadness and suffering.

Heavenly Father and His Son, Jesus Christ, want us to have joy.[2] President Russell M. Nelson has taught: "The joy we feel has little to do with the circumstances of our lives and everything to do with the focus of our lives. When the focus of our lives is on God's plan of salvation, . . . we can feel joy regardless of what is happening—or not happening—in our lives."[3]

When I was a young missionary, I remember when a marvelous missionary that I had come to admire received some devastating news. His mother and his younger brother had passed away in a tragic accident. The mission president offered this elder the option to return home for the funeral. However, after speaking with his father on the phone, this missionary decided to stay and finish his mission.

A short time later, when we were serving in the same zone, my companion and I received an emergency call; some thieves had stolen the bicycle belonging to this same missionary and had injured him with a knife. He and his companion had to walk to the nearest hospital, where my companion and I met up with them. On the way to the hospital, I was grieving for this missionary. I imagined that his spirits would be low and that surely, after this traumatic experience, he would now want to return home.

However, when we arrived at the hospital, I saw this missionary lying in his bed, waiting to be taken into surgery—and he was smiling. I thought, "How could he be smiling at a time like this?" While he was recuperating in the hospital, he enthusiastically handed out pamphlets and copies of the Book of Mormon to the doctors, nurses, and other patients. Even with these trials, he did not want to go home. Rather, he served until the last day of his mission with faith, energy, strength, and enthusiasm.

At the beginning of the Book of Mormon, Nephi states, "Having seen many afflictions in the course of my days, nevertheless, having been highly favored of the Lord in all my days."[4]

I think of the many trials that Nephi experienced, many of which are included in his writing. His trials help us understand that we all have our dark days. One of these trials occurred when Nephi was commanded to return to Jerusalem to obtain the brass plates that Laban had in his possession. Some of Nephi's brothers were men of little faith, and they even beat Nephi with a stick. Nephi experienced another trial when he broke his bow and could not obtain food for his family. Later, when Nephi was commanded to build a ship, his brothers mocked him and refused to help him. Despite these and many other trials during the course of his life, Nephi always recognized the goodness of God.

As his family was crossing the ocean on the way to the promised land, some of Nephi's family "began to make themselves merry," speak harshly, and forget that it was the Lord's power that had preserved them. When Nephi chastised them, they became offended and bound him with cords so that he was unable to move. The Book of Mormon states that his brethren "did treat [him] with much harshness"; his wrists and ankles "were much swollen, and great was the soreness."[5] Nephi was grieved with the hardness of his brothers' hearts and at times felt overcome with sorrow.[6] "Nevertheless," he declared, "I did look unto my God, and I did praise him all the day long; and I did not murmur against the Lord because of mine afflictions."[7]

My dear brothers and sisters, how do we react to our afflictions? Do we murmur before the Lord because of them? Or, like Nephi and my former missionary friend, do we feel thankful in word, thought, and deed because we are more focused on our blessings than on our problems?

Our Savior, Jesus Christ, gave us the example during His earthly ministry. In moments of difficulty and trial, there are few things that bring us greater peace and satisfaction than serving our fellow man. The book of Matthew recounts what happened when the Savior learned that His cousin John the Baptist had been beheaded by King Herod to please the daughter of Herodias:

"And his disciples came, and took up the body, and buried it, and went and told Jesus.

"When Jesus heard of it, he departed thence by ship into a desert place apart: and when the people had heard thereof, they followed him on foot out of the cities.

"And Jesus went forth, and saw a great multitude, and was moved with compassion toward them, and he healed their sick.

"And when it was evening, his disciples came to him, saying, This is a desert place, and the time is now past; send the multitude away, that they may go into the villages, and buy themselves victuals.

"But Jesus said unto them, They need not depart; give ye them to eat."[8]

Jesus Christ showed us that during times of trial and adversity, we can recognize the difficulties of others. Moved with compassion, we can reach out and lift them. And as we do so, we are

71

also lifted by our Christlike service. President Gordon B. Hinckley stated: "The best antidote I know for worry is work. The best medicine for despair is service. The best cure for weariness is the challenge of helping someone who is even more tired."[9]

In this, the Church of Jesus Christ, I have had many opportunities to minister and serve my fellow man. It is at those times when I feel that Heavenly Father lightens my burdens. President Russell M. Nelson is the prophet of God on the earth; he is a great example of how we should minister to others during difficult trials. I unite my testimony with those of many other Saints that God is our loving Heavenly Father. I have felt His infinite love during my dark days. Our Savior, Jesus Christ, understands our pains and our afflictions. He wants to ease our burdens and comfort us. We must follow His example by serving and ministering to those with even greater burdens than our own. In the name of Jesus Christ, amen.

Notes

1. See John 11:1–44.
2. See 2 Nephi 2:25.
3. Russell M. Nelson, "Joy and Spiritual Survival," *Ensign* or *Liahona*, Nov. 2016, 82.
4. 1 Nephi 1:1.
5. 1 Nephi 18:9, 11, 15.
6. See 1 Nephi 15:4–5.
7. 1 Nephi 18:16.
8. Matthew 14:12–16.
9. *Teachings of Presidents of the Church: Gordon B. Hinckley* (2016), 205.

SIMPLY BEAUTIFUL—
BEAUTIFULLY SIMPLE

ELDER GARY E. STEVENSON
Of the Quorum of the Twelve Apostles

Introduction

I offer a warm welcome to each of you participating in this conference.

Today I hope to describe two elements of the restored gospel of Jesus Christ, followed by four stirring accounts from Latter-day Saints around the world demonstrating the application of these principles. The first element of the restored gospel—God's work of salvation and exaltation—focuses on divinely appointed responsibilities. The second element reminds us that the gospel is plain, precious, and simple.

Divinely Appointed Responsibilities

To receive eternal life, we must "come unto Christ, and be perfected in him."[1] As we come unto Christ and help others do the same, we participate in God's work of salvation and exaltation, which focuses on divinely appointed responsibilities.[2] These divine responsibilities align themselves with priesthood keys restored by Moses, Elias, and Elijah, as recorded in the 110th section of the Doctrine and Covenants,[3] and the second great commandment given to us by Jesus Christ to love our neighbor as ourselves.[4] They are found on the first two pages of the updated *General Handbook*, available to all members.

If hearing the words "General Handbook" or "divinely appointed responsibilities" causes you to shudder in fear of complexity, please don't. These responsibilities are simple, inspirational, motivating, and doable. Here they are:

1. Living the gospel of Jesus Christ
2. Caring for those in need
3. Inviting all to receive the gospel
4. Uniting families for eternity

You might view them as I do: as a road map to return back to our loving Heavenly Father.

The Gospel Is Plain, Precious, and Simple

It has been said that the gospel of Jesus Christ is "simply beautiful and beautifully simple."[5] The world is not. It is complicated, complex, and filled with turmoil and strife. We are blessed as we exercise care not to allow complexity, so common in the world, to enter into the way we receive and practice the gospel.

President Dallin H. Oaks observed: "We are taught many small and simple things in the gospel of Jesus Christ. We need to be reminded that in total and over a significant period of time, those seemingly small things bring to pass great things."[6] Jesus Christ Himself describes that His yoke is easy and His burden is light.[7] We should all strive to keep the gospel simple—in our lives, in our families, in our classes and quorums, and in our wards and stakes.

As you listen to the following stories I will share with you, recognize that they have been carefully chosen to inspire on the one hand and to inform on the other. The actions of each of these Latter-day Saints becomes a model for each of us in applying the gospel in plain, precious, simple ways while fulfilling one of the divinely appointed responsibilities just introduced.

Living the Gospel of Jesus Christ

First, living the gospel of Jesus Christ. Jens of Denmark prays daily to live the gospel and notice promptings from the Holy Ghost. He has learned to act quickly when he feels directed by the Spirit.

Jens shared the following:

"We live in an idyllic, small, half-timbered house with a thatched roof, in the center of a cozy little village, close to the village pond.

"On this night with the most beautiful Danish summer weather imaginable, doors and windows were open, and everything breathed peace and quiet. Due to our gloriously bright and long summer nights, I had not been in a hurry to replace a burned-out light bulb in our utility room.

"Suddenly, I got a strong feeling that I had to replace it immediately! At the same time, I heard my wife, Mariann, call for me and the children to wash our hands because dinner was ready!

"I had been married long enough to know that this was not the time to start doing anything else than washing my hands, but I heard myself calling out to Mariann that I would just pop over to the store to buy a new light bulb. I felt a strong urge to leave immediately.

"The grocery store was only on the other side of the pond. We usually walked, but today I grabbed my bike. While riding past the pond, out of the corner of my eye I noticed a small boy, about two years old, walking alone near the edge of the pond, very close to the water—suddenly he fell in! One minute he was there—and the next he was gone!

"No one had seen this happen but me. I threw my bike on the ground, ran, and jumped into the waist-high pond. The surface of the water immediately closed with duckweed, making it impossible to see through the water. Then I sensed a movement to one side. I put my arm in the water, got hold of a T-shirt, and pulled the little boy up. He started gasping, coughing, and crying. Soon afterward the boy was reunited with his parents."

As Brother Jens prays each morning for help to recognize promptings from the Holy Ghost, even something as unusual as to immediately change a light bulb, he also prays that he can be used as a tool to bless God's children. Jens lives the gospel by seeking divine direction each day, striving to be worthy, then doing his best to follow that direction when it comes.

Caring for Those in Need

Here is an example of caring for those in need. One day a stake president in the Cúcuta stake in Colombia accompanied the stake Young Women president to visit two young women—and their older teenage brother—who were going through some terrible struggles. Recently their father had passed away, and their mother had passed away a year before. The three siblings were now left all alone in their small, humble shelter. The walls were made of crude wood lined with plastic bags, and the corrugated tin roof covered only the area where they slept.

Following their visit, these leaders knew they needed to help. Through the ward council, a plan to help them began to emerge. Ward and stake leaders—Relief Society, elders quorum, Young Men, Young Women—and many families all set themselves to the task of blessing this family.

The ward organizations contacted several ward members who work in construction. Some helped with design, others donated time and labor, others made meals, and still others donated needed materials.

When the little house was finished, it was a joyful day for those who helped and for the three young ward members. These orphaned children felt warm and reassuring bonds of their ward family to know that they are not alone and that God is always there for them. Those who reached out felt the love of the Savior for this family and acted as His hands in serving them.

Inviting All to Receive the Gospel

I think you will enjoy this example of inviting all to receive the gospel. Seventeen-year-old Cleiton of Cape Verde had no idea what would happen as a result of walking into his ward's seminary class one day. But his life and the lives of others would be forever changed because he did.

Cleiton, along with his mother and older brother, had been baptized into the Church some time earlier, and yet the family stopped attending. His single act of attending seminary would prove to be a hinge point for the family.

The other youth in the seminary class were warm and welcoming. They made Cleiton feel at home and encouraged him to attend another activity. He did so and soon began attending his other Church meetings. A wise bishop saw spiritual potential in Cleiton and invited him to be his assistant. "From that moment on," says

Bishop Cruz, "Cleiton became an example and an influence to other young people."

The first person Cleiton invited back to church was his mother, then his older brother. He then widened his circle to friends. One of those friends was a young man his own age, Wilson. Upon his very first meeting with the missionaries, Wilson expressed his desire to be baptized. The missionaries were impressed and amazed at how much Cleiton had already shared with Wilson.

Cleiton's efforts didn't stop there. He helped other less-active members return, in addition to sharing the gospel with friends of other faiths. Today the ward has 35 active youth, with a thriving seminary program, thanks in large part to Cleiton's efforts to love, share, and invite. Cleiton and his older brother, Cléber, are both preparing to serve full-time missions.

Uniting Families for Eternity

Finally, let me share a beautiful example of uniting families for eternity. Lydia from Kharkiv, Ukraine, first learned about the temple from the missionaries. Immediately, Lydia felt a fervent desire to attend the temple, and after her baptism, she began preparation to receive a temple recommend.

Lydia attended the Freiberg Germany Temple to receive her endowment and then spent several days doing proxy work there. Following the dedication of the Kyiv Ukraine Temple, Lydia attended the temple more frequently. She and her husband, Anatoly, were eternally sealed there and later called to serve as temple missionaries. Together they have found more than 15,000 names of ancestors and have worked to provide temple ordinances for them.

When asked about her feelings regarding temple work, Lydia says, "What did I receive in the temple? I have made new covenants with God. My testimony has been strengthened. I have learned to receive personal revelation. I am able to perform saving ordinances for my deceased ancestors. And I can love and serve other people." She concluded with this very true statement: "The Lord wants to see us in the temple often."

Conclusion

I am inspired by the goodness of these Latter-day Saints, each with diverse and varied backgrounds, centered in these four stories. Much can be learned from miraculous outcomes brought through the simple application of simple gospel principles. All they did is within our grasp as well.

May we keep the gospel simple as we take upon us our divinely appointed responsibilities: To *live the gospel of Jesus Christ* so as to be sensitive to promptings, as did Jens in Denmark. To *care for those in need*, as demonstrated by the members of the Cúcuta stake in Colombia in providing shelter to orphaned ward members. To *invite all to receive the gospel*, in the way that Cleiton from the African island country of Cape Verde did with his friends and family. Finally, to *unite families for eternity*, as exemplified by Sister Lydia from Ukraine through her own temple ordinances, family history efforts, and service in the temple.

Doing so will surely bring joy and peace. Of this I promise and testify—and of Jesus Christ as our Savior and our Redeemer—in the name of Jesus Christ, amen.

Notes

1. Moroni 10:32.
2. See *General Handbook: Serving in The Church of Jesus Christ of Latter-day Saints*, 1.2, ChurchofJesusChrist.org.
3. See Doctrine and Covenants 110:11–16. See also Dallin H. Oaks, "The Melchizedek Priesthood and the Keys," *Ensign* or *Liahona*, May 2020, 70: "Following the dedication of the first temple of this dispensation in Kirtland, Ohio, three prophets—Moses, Elias, and Elijah—restored 'the keys of this dispensation,' including keys pertaining to the gathering of Israel and the work of the temples of the Lord." See also Quentin L. Cook, "Prepare to Meet God," *Ensign* or *Liahona*, May 2018, 114: "Ancient prophets restored priesthood keys for the eternal saving ordinances of the gospel of Jesus Christ. . . . These keys provide the 'power from on high' [Doctrine and Covenants 38:38] for divinely appointed responsibilities that constitute the primary purpose of the Church."
4. See Matthew 22:36–40.
5. In *Matthew Cowley Speaks: Discourses of Elder Matthew Cowley of the Quorum of the Twelve of The Church of Jesus Christ of Latter-day Saints* (1954), xii.
6. Dallin H. Oaks, "Small and Simple Things," *Ensign* or *Liahona*, May 2018, 89.
7. See Matthew 11:30.

SATURDAY EVENING SESSION

OCTOBER 2, 2021

"LOVEST THOU ME MORE THAN THESE?"

PRESIDENT M. RUSSELL BALLARD
Acting President of the Quorum of the Twelve Apostles

In November 2019, my friend and I visited the Holy Land. While there, we reviewed and studied scriptures about Jesus Christ's life. One morning we stood on the northwestern shore of the Sea of Galilee at a place that may have been where Jesus met His disciples following His Resurrection.

After Jesus's Resurrection, as we read in John chapter 21, Peter and the other disciples fished all night without success.[1] In the morning, they saw a man standing on the shore who told them to cast their net on the other side of the boat. To their astonishment, the net was filled miraculously.[2]

They immediately recognized that the man was the Lord, and they rushed to greet Him.

As they dragged the net to shore, full of fish, Jesus said, "Come and dine."[3] John reports that "when they had dined, Jesus saith to Simon Peter, Simon, son of Jonas, *lovest thou me more than these?*"[4]

While I was standing on that same seashore, I realized that the Savior's question was one of the most important questions that He might someday ask me. I could almost hear His voice asking, "Russell, lovest thou me more than these?"

Do you wonder what Jesus was referring to when He asked Peter, "Lovest thou me more than these?"

Relating this question to ourselves in our day, the Lord may be asking us about how busy we are and about the many positive and negative influences competing for our attention and our time. He may be asking each of us if we love Him more than the things of this world. This may be a question about what we really value in life, who we follow, and how we view our relationships with family members and neighbors. Or maybe He is asking what really brings us joy and happiness.

Do the things of this world bring us the joy, happiness, and peace that the Savior offered to His disciples and that He offers to us? Only He can bring us true joy, happiness, and peace through our loving Him and following His teachings.

How would we answer the question "Lovest thou me more than these?"

When we discover a fuller meaning of this question, we can become better family members, neighbors, citizens, members of the Church, and sons and daughters of God.

At my age, I have attended many funerals. I am sure many of you have noticed what I have noticed. When celebrating the life of a deceased family member or a friend, it is rare for the speaker to talk about the size of the person's home, the number of cars, or the bank account balances. They usually don't speak about social media posts. At most of the funerals that I have attended, they focus on their loved one's relationships, service to others, life lessons and experiences, and their love for Jesus Christ.

Don't misunderstand me. I'm not saying that having a nice home or a nice car is wrong or that using social media is bad. What I *am* saying is that in the end, those things matter very little compared to loving the Savior.

When we love and follow Him, we have faith in Him. We repent. We follow His example and are baptized and receive the Holy Ghost. We endure to the end and stay on the covenant path. We forgive family members and neighbors by letting go of grudges we may be holding. We earnestly strive to keep God's commandments. We strive to be obedient. We make and keep covenants. We honor our fathers and mothers. We set aside negative worldly influences. We prepare ourselves for His Second Coming.

In "The Living Christ: The Testimony of the Apostles," we read: "[Jesus] will someday return to earth. . . . He will rule as King of Kings and reign as Lord of Lords, and every knee shall bend and every tongue shall speak in worship before Him. Each of us will stand to be judged of Him according to our works and the desires of our hearts."[5]

As one of the Apostles who signed "The Living Christ" document, I can say that knowing that Jesus "is the light, the life, and the hope of the world"[6] gives me a greater desire to love Him more every day.

I testify that Heavenly Father and Jesus Christ live. I testify that They love us. The scriptures teach that "God so loved the world, that he gave his only begotten Son, that whosoever believeth in him should not perish, but have everlasting life."[7] The scriptures also teach that Jesus "so loved the world that he gave his own life, that as many as would believe might become the sons [and daughters] of God."[8]

Heavenly Father so loved us that He prepared His plan of salvation with a Savior as the central figure. And Jesus so loved us that in the great Council in Heaven, when Heavenly Father asked, "Whom shall I send?" Jesus, who was the firstborn of all the Father's spirit children, answered, "Here am I, send me."[9] He said unto the Father, "Father, thy will be done, and the glory be thine forever."[10] Jesus volunteered to be our Savior and Redeemer so that we could become like Them and return to Their presence.

These two scriptures also teach that to return to Their presence we need to *believe*. We need to believe in Jesus and in God's plan of happiness. To *believe* is to love and follow our Savior and keep the commandments, even in the midst of trials and strife.

Today's world is unsettled. There are disappointments, disagreements, distress, and distractions.

President Dallin H. Oaks, speaking in 2017, noted the following: "These are challenging times, filled with big worries: wars and rumors of wars, possible epidemics of infectious diseases, droughts, floods, and global warming."[11]

We cannot lose our love for and hope in Jesus, even if we face seemingly overwhelming challenges. Heavenly Father and Jesus will never forget us. They love us.

Last October, President Russell M. Nelson taught us the importance of putting Heavenly Father and Jesus Christ first in our lives. President Nelson taught us that one meaning of the word *Israel* is "let God prevail."[12]

He asked each of us these questions: "Are *you* willing to let God prevail in your life? Are *you* willing to let God be the most important influence in your life? Will you allow His words, His commandments, and His covenants to influence what you do each day? Will you allow His voice to take priority over any other? Are you *willing* to let whatever He needs you to do take precedence over every other ambition? Are you *willing* to have your will swallowed up in His?"[13]

We must always remember that our true happiness depends upon our relationship with God, with Jesus Christ, and with each other.

One way to demonstrate our love is by joining family, friends, and neighbors in doing some small things to better serve each other. Do things that make this world a better place.

What things can you do within your own life to show that you love the Lord first?

As we focus on loving our neighbors as He loves them, we start to truly love those around us.[14]

I ask again, how would you respond to the Savior's question "Lovest thou me more than these?"

As you consider this question, as I have done, I pray that you may answer as Peter did so long ago, "Yea, Lord; thou knowest that I love thee,"[15] and then show it by loving and serving God and all those around you.

I testify that we are blessed to have the gospel of Jesus Christ to guide us in the way we live and treat each other. In Him, we discover that every daughter and son of God is very precious to Him.

I testify that Jesus Christ is our beloved Savior. He is the Only Begotten Son of God. And I bear this testimony humbly in the name of Jesus Christ, amen.

Notes

1. See John 21:3.
2. See John 21:11.
3. John 21:12.
4. John 21:15; emphasis added.
5. "The Living Christ: The Testimony of the Apostles," ChurchofJesusChrist.org.
6. "The Living Christ," ChurchofJesusChrist.org.
7. John 3:16.
8. Doctrine and Covenants 34:3.
9. Abraham 3:27.

10. Moses 4:2.
11. Dallin H. Oaks, "Push Back against the World" (Brigham Young University–Hawaii commencement address, Feb. 25, 2017), speeches.byuh.edu.
12. Russell M. Nelson, "Let God Prevail," *Ensign* or *Liahona*, Nov. 2020, 92; see also Bible Dictionary, "Israel."
13. Russell M. Nelson, "Let God Prevail," 94.
14. See John 15:12–13; Ephesians 5:1–2; 1 John 3:2–3, 16–18, 23–24; 4:7, 9–11, 20–21; Moses 1:39.
15. John 21:15.

I PRAY HE'LL USE US

SHARON EUBANK

First Counselor in the Relief Society General Presidency

This cookie made of phyllo dough and pistachio nuts is a thank-you. It was made by the Kadado family who, for decades, owned three bakeries in Damascus, Syria. When war came, a blockade stopped food and supplies from reaching their part of the city. The Kadados began to starve. At the height of this desperate situation, Latter-day Saint Charities and some very courageous staff at Rahma Worldwide began serving a daily hot meal, along with milk for the little children. After a difficult time, the family began their life—as well as their bakery—once again in a new country.

Recently, a box of cookies arrived at the Church offices with the following message: "For more than two months, we managed to get food from the Rahma–Latter-day Saint [Charities] kitchen. Without it we would [have] starve[d] to death. Please accept this . . . sample from my shop as a small token of thanks. I ask God the Almighty to bless you . . . in everything you do."[1]

A cookie of gratitude and remembrance. It is meant for you. To all who prayed after watching a story on the news, to all who volunteered when it was not convenient or who kindly donated money to the humanitarian fund trusting it would do some good, thank you.

Divine Responsibility to Care for the Poor

The Church of Jesus Christ is under divine mandate to care for the poor.[2] It is one of the pillars of the work of salvation and exaltation.[3] What was true during the days of Alma is certainly true for us: "And thus, in their prosperous circumstances, they did not send away any who were naked, or that were hungry, or that were athirst, or that were sick, or that had not been nourished; and they did not set their hearts upon riches; therefore they were liberal to all, both old and young, both bond and free, both male and female, whether out of the church or in the church, having no respect to persons as to those who stood in need."[4]

The Church responds to this charge in a wide variety of ways, including:

- the ministering we do through Relief Society, priesthood quorums, and classes;
- fasting and the use of fast offerings;
- welfare farms and canneries;
- welcome centers for immigrants;
- outreach for those in prison;
- Church humanitarian efforts;
- and the JustServe app, where it's available, that matches volunteers with service opportunities.

These are all ways, organized through the priesthood, where small efforts collectively make a big impact, magnifying the many individual things we do as disciples of Jesus Christ.

Prophets Have Stewardship for the Whole Earth

Prophets have charge for the whole earth, not just for members of the Church. I can report from my own experience how personally and devotedly the First Presidency takes that charge. As needs grow, the First Presidency has charged us to increase our humanitarian outreach in a significant way. They are interested in the largest trends and the smallest details.

Recently, we brought to them one of the protective medical gowns that Beehive Clothing sewed for hospitals to use during the pandemic. As a medical doctor, President Russell M. Nelson was highly interested. He didn't want to just see it. He wanted to try it on—check the cuffs and the length and the way it tied in the back. He told us later, with emotion in his voice, "When you meet with people on your assignments, thank them for their fasting, their offerings, and their ministering in the name of the Lord."

Humanitarian Report

At President Nelson's direction, I am reporting back to you about how The Church of Jesus Christ of Latter-day Saints is responding to hurricanes, earthquakes, refugee displacement—and even a pandemic—thanks to the kindness of the Latter-day Saints and many friends. While the more than 1,500 COVID-19 projects were certainly the largest focus of the Church's relief over the last 18 months, the Church also responded to 933 natural disasters and refugee crises in 108 countries. But statistics don't tell the whole story. Let me share four brief examples to illustrate the smallest taste of what is being done.

South African COVID Relief

Sixteen-year-old Dieke Mphuti of Welkom, South Africa, lost her parents years ago, leaving her to care for three younger siblings on her own. It was always daunting for her to find enough food, but COVID supply shortages and quarantines made it almost impossible. They were often hungry, scraping by only with the generosity of neighbors.

On a sunny day in August 2020, Dieke was surprised by a knock at her door. She opened it to find two strangers—one a Church representative from the area office in Johannesburg and the other an official from South Africa's Department of Social Development.

The two organizations had teamed up to bring food to at-risk households. Relief washed over Dieke as she glimpsed the pile of cornmeal and other food staples, purchased with Church humanitarian funds. These would help her to sustain her family for several weeks until a government aid package could begin to take effect for her.

Dieke's story is one of thousands of such experiences taking place across the world during the COVID pandemic thanks to your consecrated contributions.

Afghan Relief at Ramstein

We have all seen recent images in the news: thousands of evacuees being flown from Afghanistan. Many arrived at air bases or other temporary locations in Qatar, the United States, Germany, and Spain before continuing to their final destinations. Their needs were immediate, and the Church responded with supplies and volunteers.

At Ramstein Air Base in Germany, the Church provided large donations of diapers, baby formula, food, and shoes.

Some of the Relief Society sisters noticed that many Afghan women were using their husbands' shirts to cover their heads because their traditional head coverings had been ripped off in the frenzy at the Kabul airport. In an act of friendship that crossed any religious or cultural boundaries, the sisters of the Ramstein First Ward gathered to sew traditional Muslim clothing for Afghan women. Sister Bethani Halls said, "We heard that women were in need of prayer garments, and we are sewing so that they can be [comfortable] for prayer."[5]

Haitian Earthquake Relief

This next example shows you do not have to be wealthy or old to be an instrument for good. Eighteen-year-old Marie "Djadjou" Jacques is from the Cavaillon Branch in Haiti. When the devastating earthquake struck near her town in August, her family's house was one of tens of thousands of buildings that collapsed. It's almost impossible to imagine the despair of losing your home. But rather than giving in to that despair, Djadjou—incredibly—turned outward.

She saw an elderly neighbor struggling and began taking care of her. She helped others clear away debris. Despite her exhaustion, she joined other Church members to distribute food and hygiene kits to others. Djadjou's story is just one of many powerful examples of service carried out by youth and young adults as they strive to follow the example of Jesus Christ.

German Flood Relief

Only a few weeks before the earthquake, another group of young adults was giving similar service across the Atlantic. The floods that swept through western Europe in July were the most severe in decades.

When the waters finally receded, one shopkeeper in the riverside district of Ahrweiler, Germany, surveyed the damage and was utterly overwhelmed. This humble man, a devout Catholic, whispered a prayer that God might send someone to help him. The very next morning, President Dan Hammon of the Germany Frankfurt Mission arrived on the street with a small band of missionaries wearing yellow Helping Hands vests. The water had reached up to 10 feet (3 m) on the shopkeeper's walls, leaving behind a deep layer of mud. The volunteers shoveled out the mud, removed the carpet and drywall, and piled everything in the street for removal. The overjoyed shopkeeper worked alongside them for hours, amazed that the Lord had sent a group of His servants to answer his prayer—and within 24 hours![6]

"Well, I Pray That He'll Use Us"

Speaking of the Church's humanitarian efforts, Elder Jeffrey R. Holland once remarked: "Prayers are answered . . . most of the time . . . by God using other people. Well, I pray that He'll use us. I pray that we'll be the answer to people's prayers."[7]

Brothers and sisters, through your ministry, donations, time, and love, you have been the answer to so many prayers. And yet there is so much more to do. As baptized members of the Church, we are under covenant to care for those in need. Our individual efforts don't necessarily require money or faraway locations;[8] they do require the guidance of the Holy Spirit and a willing heart to say to the Lord, "Here am I; send me."[9]

The Acceptable Year of the Lord

Luke 4 records that Jesus came to Nazareth, where He had been brought up, and stood up in the synagogue to read. This was near the beginning of His mortal ministry, and He quoted a passage from the book of Isaiah:

"The Spirit of the Lord is upon me, because he hath anointed me to preach the gospel to the poor; he hath sent me to heal the brokenhearted, to preach deliverance to the captives, and recovering of sight to the blind, to set at liberty them that are bruised,

"To preach the acceptable year of the Lord. . . .

". . . This day is this scripture fulfilled in your ears."[10]

I testify that the scripture is being fulfilled in our own time as well. I testify Jesus Christ is come to heal the brokenhearted. His gospel is to recover sight to the blind. His Church is to preach deliverance to the captive, and His disciples across the world are striving to set at liberty them that are bruised.

Let me conclude by repeating the question Jesus asked His Apostle Simon Peter: "Do you love me?"[11] The essence of the gospel is contained in how we answer that question for ourselves and "feed [His] sheep."[12] With great reverence and love for Jesus Christ, our Master, I invite each of us to be a part of His magnificent ministry, and I pray He'll use us. In the sacred name of Jesus Christ, amen.

Notes

1. Abdul Razaq, personal correspondence, May 2021.
2. See Doctrine and Covenants 104:11–18.
3. See *General Handbook: Serving in The Church of Jesus Christ of Latter-day Saints*, 1.2.2, ChurchofJesusChrist.org.
4. Alma 1:30.
5. Bethani Halls, quoted in "Aiding Afghan Evacuees," Europe Area Welfare and Self-Reliance Newsletter, Aug. 2021.
6. From Dan Hammon (Germany Frankfurt Mission president), email to Ty Johnson, 2021.
7. Jeffrey R. Holland, "Neonatal Resuscitation with Elder Holland" (video), The Church of Jesus Christ of Latter-day Saints, Nov. 10, 2011, youtube.com.
8. See Sharon Eubank, "16 Things You Can Do to Be a Humanitarian," Oct. 3, 2021, ChurchofJesusChrist.org.
9. Isaiah 6:8; see also Abraham 3:27.
10. Luke 4:18–19, 21.
11. See John 21:15–17.
12. John 21:15–17.

IS THERE NO BALM IN GILEAD?

ELDER BRENT H. NIELSON
Of the Presidency of the Seventy

Shortly after my mission, while a student at Brigham Young University, I received a phone call from my dad. He told me that he had been diagnosed with pancreatic cancer and that although his chances of survival were not good, he was determined to be healed and return to his normal life activities. That phone call was a sobering moment for me. My dad had been my bishop, my friend, and my adviser. As my mother, my siblings, and I contemplated the future, it appeared bleak. My younger brother, Dave, was serving a mission in New York and participated long-distance in these difficult family events.

The medical providers of the day suggested surgery to try and curtail the spread of the cancer. Our family earnestly fasted and prayed for a miracle. I felt that we had sufficient faith that my father could be healed. Just prior to the surgery, my older brother, Norm, and I gave my dad a blessing. With all the faith we could muster, we prayed that he would be healed.

The surgery was scheduled to last many hours, but after just a short time, the doctor came to the waiting room to meet with our family. He told us that as they began the surgery, they could see that the cancer had spread throughout my father's body. Based upon what they observed, my father had just a few months to live. We were devastated.

As my father awakened from the surgery, he was anxious to learn if the procedure had been successful. We shared with him the grim news.

We continued to fast and pray for a miracle. As my father's health quickly declined, we began to pray that he could be free of pain. Eventually, as his condition worsened, we asked the Lord to allow him to pass quickly. Just a few months after the surgery, as predicted by the surgeon, my father did pass away.

Much love and care were poured out upon our family by ward

members and family friends. We had a beautiful funeral that honored the life of my father. As time passed, however, and we experienced the pain of my father's absence, I began to wonder why my father had not been healed. I wondered if my faith was not strong enough. Why did some families receive a miracle, but our family did not? I had learned on my mission to turn to the scriptures for answers, so I began to search the scriptures.

The Old Testament teaches of an aromatic spice or ointment used for healing wounds that was made from a bush grown in Gilead. In Old Testament times, the ointment came to be known as the "balm of Gilead."[1] The prophet Jeremiah lamented over the calamities that he observed among his people and hoped for healing. Jeremiah questioned, "Is there no balm in Gilead; is there no physician there?"[2] Through literature, music, and art, the Savior Jesus Christ has often been referred to as the Balm of Gilead because of His remarkable healing power. Like Jeremiah, I was wondering, "Is there no balm in Gilead for the Nielson family?"

In Mark chapter 2 of the New Testament, we find the Savior in Capernaum. Word of the Savior's healing power had spread throughout the land, and many people traveled to Capernaum to be healed by the Savior. There were so many gathered around the house where the Savior was located that there was no room for Him to receive them all. Four men carried a man sick of the palsy to be healed by the Savior. They were unable to make their way through the crowd, and so they uncovered the roof of the house and lowered the man down to meet the Savior.

As I read this account, I was surprised by what the Savior said as He met this man: "Son, thy sins be forgiven thee."[3] I thought that if I had been one of the four men who had carried this man, I might have said to the Savior, "We actually brought him here to be healed." I think the Savior might have replied, "I did heal him." Was it possible that I had not fully understood—that the Savior's healing power was not just His ability to heal our bodies but, perhaps even more important, His ability to heal our hearts and the broken hearts of my family?

The Savior taught an important lesson through this experience as He eventually physically healed the man. It became clear to me that His message was that He could touch the eyes of those who were blind, and they could see. He could touch the ears of those who were deaf, and they could hear. He could touch the legs of those who could not walk, and they could walk. He can heal our eyes and our ears and our legs, but most important of all, He can heal our hearts as He cleanses us from sin and lifts us through difficult trials.

When the Savior appears to the people in the Book of Mormon after His Resurrection, He again speaks of His healing power. The Nephites hear His voice from heaven saying, "Will ye not now return unto me, and repent of your sins, and be converted, *that I may heal you?*"[4] Later, the Savior teaches, "For ye know not but what they will return and repent, and come unto me with full purpose of heart, and *I shall heal them.*"[5] The Savior was not referring to a physical healing but rather a spiritual healing of their souls.

Moroni brings additional understanding as he shares the words of his father, Mormon. After speaking of miracles, Mormon explains, "And Christ hath said: If ye will have faith in me ye shall have power to do whatsoever thing is expedient in me."[6] I learned that the object of my faith must be Jesus Christ and that I needed to accept what was expedient to Him as I exercised faith in Him. I understand now that my father's passing was expedient to God's plan. Now, as I lay my hands upon the head of another to bless him or her, my faith is in Jesus Christ, and I understand that a person can and will be physically healed if it is expedient in Christ.

The Savior's Atonement, which makes available both His redeeming and His enabling power, is the ultimate blessing that Jesus Christ offers to all. As we repent with full purpose of heart, the Savior cleanses us from sin. As we cheerfully submit our will to the Father, even in the most difficult of circumstances, the Savior will lift our burdens and make them light.[7]

But here is the greater lesson I learned. I had mistakenly believed that the Savior's healing power had not worked for my family. As I now look back with more mature eyes and experience, I see that the Savior's healing power was evident in the lives of each of my family members. I was so focused on a physical healing that I failed to see the miracles that had occurred. The Lord strengthened and lifted my mother beyond her capacity through this difficult trial, and she led a long and productive life. She had a remarkable positive influence on her children and grandchildren. The Lord blessed me and my siblings with love, unity, faith, and resilience that became an important part of our lives and continues today.

But what about my dad? As with all who will repent, he was spiritually healed as he sought and received the blessings available because of the Savior's Atonement. He received a remission of his sins and now awaits the miracle of the Resurrection. The Apostle Paul taught, "For as in Adam all die, even so in Christ shall all be made alive."[8] You see, I was saying to the Savior, "We brought my dad to You to be healed," and it is now clear to me that the Savior did heal him. The balm of Gilead worked for the Nielson family—not in the way that we had supposed, but in an even more significant way that has blessed and continues to bless our lives.

In John chapter 6 of the New Testament, the Savior performed a most interesting miracle. With just a few fish and a few loaves of bread, the Savior fed 5,000. I have read this account many times, but there is a part of that experience I missed that now has great meaning to me. After the Savior fed 5,000, He asked His disciples to gather up the remaining fragments, the leftovers, which filled 12 baskets. I have wondered why the Savior took the time to do that. It has become clear to me that one lesson we can learn from that occasion was this: He could feed 5,000 and there were leftovers. "My grace is sufficient for all men."[9] The Savior's redeeming and healing power can cover any sin, wound, or trial—no matter how large or how difficult—and there are leftovers. His grace is sufficient.

With that knowledge, we can move forward with faith, knowing that when difficult times come—and they surely will—or when sin encompasses our lives, the Savior stands "with healing in his wings,"[10] inviting us to come unto Him.

I bear my witness to you of the Balm of Gilead, the Savior Jesus Christ, our Redeemer, and of His marvelous healing power. I bear my witness of His desire to heal you. In the name of Jesus Christ, amen.

Notes

1. See Bible Dictionary, "Balm."
2. Jeremiah 8:22.
3. Mark 2:5.
4. 3 Nephi 9:13; emphasis added.
5. 3 Nephi 18:32; emphasis added.
6. Moroni 7:33.
7. See Mosiah 24:15.
8. 1 Corinthians 15:22.
9. Ether 12:27.
10. Malachi 4:2.

DEEPENING OUR CONVERSION TO JESUS CHRIST

ELDER ARNULFO VALENZUELA
Of the Seventy

My dear brothers and sisters, President Russell M. Nelson has taught us recently: "To do anything well requires effort. Becoming a true disciple of Jesus Christ is no exception. Increasing your faith and trust in Him takes effort." Among the recommendations that he gave us to increase our faith in Jesus Christ is that we become engaged learners, that we immerse ourselves in the scriptures to understand better Christ's mission and ministry. (See "Christ Is Risen; Faith in Him Will Move Mountains," *Liahona*, May 2021, 103.)

We learn in the Book of Mormon that the scriptures were an important part of Lehi's family—so much so that Nephi and his brothers returned to Jerusalem to obtain the plates of brass (see 1 Nephi 3–4).

The scriptures reveal God's will for us, much as the Liahona did for Nephi and his father. After he broke his bow, Nephi needed to know where he should go to obtain food. His father, Lehi, looked at the Liahona and saw the things that were written. Nephi saw that the spindles functioned according to the faith, diligence, and attention given to them. He also saw writing which was easy to read and which gave them understanding regarding the paths of the Lord. He became aware that the Lord brings about great things through small means. He was obedient regarding the directions given by the Liahona. He went up the mountain and obtained food for his family, who had suffered so much from the lack thereof. (See 1 Nephi 16:23–31.)

It seems to me that Nephi was a student dedicated to the scriptures. We read that Nephi delighted in the scriptures, pondered them in his heart, and wrote them for the learning and profit of his children (see 2 Nephi 4:15–16).

President Russell M. Nelson said:

"If we 'press forward, feasting upon the word of Christ, and endure to the end, . . . [we] shall have eternal life' [2 Nephi 31:20].

"To feast means more than to taste. To feast means to savor. We savor the scriptures by studying them in a spirit of delightful discovery and faithful obedience. When we feast upon the words of Christ, they are embedded 'in fleshy tables of the heart' [2 Corinthians 3:3]. They become an integral part of our nature" ("Living by Scriptural Guidance," *Ensign*, Nov. 2000, 17; *Liahona*, Jan. 2001, 21).

What Are Some of the Things That We Will Do If Our Souls Delight in the Scriptures?

Our desire to be part of the gathering of Israel on both sides of the veil will increase. It will be normal and natural for us to invite our family and friends to listen to the missionaries. We will be worthy, and we will have a current temple recommend in order to go to the temple as often as possible. We will work to find, prepare, and submit the names of our ancestors to the temple. We will be faithful in keeping the Sabbath day, attending church every Sunday to renew our covenants with the Lord as we participate worthily in taking the sacrament. We will resolve to remain on the covenant path, living by every word that proceeds forth from the mouth of God (see Doctrine and Covenants 84:44).

What Does It Mean for You to Delight in the Things of the Lord?

Delighting in the scriptures is more than hungering and thirsting for knowledge. Nephi experienced great joy during his life. However, he also faced difficulties and sadness (see 2 Nephi 4:12–13). "Nevertheless," he said, "I know in whom I have trusted" (2 Nephi 4:19). As we study the scriptures, we will better understand God's plan of salvation and exaltation, and we will trust in the promises that He has made to us in the scriptures, as well as in the promises and blessings of modern prophets.

One afternoon, my wife and I were invited to a home of a friend. Their seven-year-old son, David, had never heard the Bible story of David and Goliath, and he wanted to hear it. As I began to tell the story, he was touched by the way David, with his faith and in the name of the God of Israel, wounded and killed the Philistine with a sling and a stone, having no sword in his hand (see 1 Samuel 17).

Looking at me with his enormous dark eyes, he asked me firmly, "Who is God?" I explained to him that God is our Heavenly Father and that we learn about Him in the scriptures.

Then he asked me, "What are the scriptures?" I told him that the scriptures are the word of God and that in them he would find beautiful stories that would help him to better know God. I asked his mother to use the Bible that she had in her home and that she not let David go to sleep without reading the whole story to him. He was delighted as he listened to it. The scriptures and our knowledge of God are gifts—gifts that we too often take for granted. Let us cherish these blessings.

While serving a mission as a young man, I observed that by our teaching with the scriptures, the lives of many people were transformed. I became aware of the power in them and how they can change our lives. Each person to whom we taught the restored gospel was a unique individual with different needs. The holy scriptures—yes, the prophecies written by the holy prophets—brought them to a faith in the Lord and to repentance and changed their hearts.

The scriptures filled them with joy as they received inspiration, direction, consolation, strength, and answers to their needs. Many of them decided to make changes in their lives and began to keep God's commandments.

Nephi encourages us to delight in the words of Christ, because the words of Christ will tell us all the things we need to do (see 2 Nephi 32:3).

I invite you to have a permanent plan to study the scriptures. *Come, Follow Me* is a great resource that we have for teaching and learning the gospel, deepening our conversion to Jesus Christ, and helping us to become like Him. When we study the gospel, we are not simply seeking new information; rather, we are seeking to become "a new creature" (2 Corinthians 5:17).

The Holy Ghost guides us toward truth and testifies to us of the truth (see John 16:13). He illuminates our minds and renews our understanding and touches our hearts through God's revelation, the source of all truth. The Holy Ghost purifies our hearts. He inspires in us the desire to live according to the truth and whispers to us ways to do so. "The Holy Ghost . . . shall teach you all things" (John 14:26).

Speaking of the words He revealed to the Prophet Joseph Smith, our Savior said:

"These words are not of men nor of man, but of me; . . .

"For it is my voice which speaketh them unto you; for they are given by my Spirit unto you . . . ;

"Wherefore, you can testify that you have heard my voice, and know my words" (Doctrine and Covenants 18:34–36).

We should seek the companionship of the Holy Ghost. This goal should govern our decisions and guide our thoughts and actions. We must seek everything that invites the influence of the Spirit and reject anything that deviates from this influence.

I testify that Jesus Christ is the beloved Son of our Heavenly Father. I love my Savior. I am grateful for His scriptures and for His living prophets. President Nelson is His prophet. In the name of Jesus Christ, amen.

WORTHINESS IS NOT FLAWLESSNESS

BRADLEY R. WILCOX

Second Counselor in the Young Men General Presidency

I once sent a message to my daughter and son-in-law using the voice-to-text feature on my phone. I said, "Hey, you two. Sure love you." They received, "Hate you two. Should love you." Isn't it amazing how easily a positive and well-intentioned message can be misunderstood? This is what sometimes happens with God's messages of repentance and worthiness.

Some mistakenly receive the message that repentance and change are unnecessary. God's message is that they are essential.[1] But doesn't God love us despite our shortcomings? Of course! He loves us perfectly. I love my grandchildren, imperfections and all, but that does not mean I don't want them to improve and become all they can become. God loves us as we are, but He also loves us too much to leave us this way.[2] Growing up unto the Lord is what mortality is all about.[3] Change is what Christ's Atonement is all about. Not only can Christ resurrect, cleanse, console, and heal us, but through it all, He can transform us to become more like Him.[4]

Some mistakenly receive the message that repentance is a one-time event. God's message is that, as President Russell M. Nelson has taught, "Repentance . . . is a process."[5] Repentance may take time and repeated effort,[6] so forsaking sin[7] and having "no more disposition to do evil, but to do good continually"[8] are lifetime pursuits.[9]

Life is like a cross-country road trip. We can't reach our destination on one tank of gas. We must refill the tank over and over. Taking the sacrament is like pulling into the gas station. As we repent and renew our covenants, we pledge our willingness to keep the commandments, and God and Christ bless us with the Holy Spirit.[10] In short, we promise to press forward on our journey, and God and Christ promise to refill the tank.

Some mistakenly receive the message that they are not worthy to participate fully in the gospel because they are not completely free of bad habits. God's message is that worthiness is not flawlessness.[11]

Worthiness is being honest and trying. We must be honest with God, priesthood leaders, and others who love us,[12] and we must strive to keep God's commandments and never give up just because we slip up.[13] Elder Bruce C. Hafen said that developing a Christlike character "requires patience and persistence more than it requires flawlessness."[14] The Lord has said the gifts of the Spirit are "given for the benefit of those who love me and keep all my commandments, *and him that seeketh so to do.*"[15]

One young man I'll call Damon wrote: "Growing up, I struggled with pornography. I always felt so ashamed that I could not get things right." Each time Damon slipped, the pain of regret became so intense, he harshly judged himself to be unworthy of any kind of grace, forgiveness, or additional chances from God. He said: "I decided I just deserved to feel terrible all the time. I figured God probably hated me because I wasn't willing to work harder and get on top of this once and for all. I would go a week and sometimes even a month, but then I would relapse and think, 'I'll never be good enough, so what's the use of even trying?'"

At one such low moment, Damon said to his priesthood leader: "Maybe I should just stop coming to church. I'm sick of being a hypocrite."

His leader responded: "You're not a hypocrite because you have a bad habit you are trying to break. You are a hypocrite if you hide it, lie about it, or try to convince yourself the Church has the problem for maintaining such high standards. Being honest about your actions and taking steps to move forward is not being a hypocrite. It is being a disciple."[16] This leader quoted Elder Richard G. Scott, who taught: "The Lord sees weaknesses differently than He does rebellion. . . . When the Lord speaks of weaknesses, it is always with mercy."[17]

That perspective gave Damon hope. He realized God was not up there saying, "Damon blew it again." Instead, He was probably saying, "Look how far Damon has come." This young man finally stopped looking down in shame or looking sideways for excuses and rationalizations. He looked up for divine help, and he found it.[18]

Damon said: "The only time I had turned to God in the past was to ask for forgiveness, but now I also asked for grace—His 'enabling power' [Bible Dictionary, "Grace"]. I had never done that before. These days I spend a lot less time hating myself for what I have done and a lot more time loving Jesus for what He has done."

Considering how long Damon had struggled, it was unhelpful and unrealistic for parents and leaders assisting him to say "never again" too quickly or to arbitrarily set some standard of abstinence to be considered "worthy." Instead, they started with small, reachable goals. They got rid of the all-or-nothing expectations and focused on incremental growth, which allowed Damon to build on a series of successes instead of failures.[19] He, like the enslaved people of Limhi, learned he could "prosper by degrees."[20]

Elder D. Todd Christofferson has counseled: "To deal with something [very] big, we may need to work at it in small, daily bites. . . . Incorporating new and wholesome habits into our character or overcoming bad habits or addictions [most] often means an effort today followed by another tomorrow and then another, perhaps for many days, even months and years. . . . But we can do it because we can appeal to God . . . for the help we need each day."[21]

Now, brothers and sisters, the COVID-19 pandemic has not been easy for anyone, but the isolation associated with quarantine restrictions has made life especially difficult for those struggling with bad habits. Remember change is possible, repentance is a process, and worthiness is not flawlessness. Most important, remember that God and Christ are willing to help us right here and now.[22]

Some mistakenly receive the message that God is waiting to help until *after* we repent. God's message is that He will help us *as* we repent. His grace is available to us "no matter where we are in the path of obedience."[23] Elder Dieter F. Uchtdorf has said: "God does not need people who are flawless. He seeks those who will offer their 'heart and a willing mind' [Doctrine and Covenants 64:34], and He will make them 'perfect in Christ' [Moroni 10:32–33]."[24]

So many have been hurt by broken and strained relationships that it is difficult for them to believe in God's compassion and long-suffering. They struggle to see God as He is—a loving Father who meets us in our need[25] and knows how to "give good things to them that ask him."[26] His grace is not just a prize for the worthy. It is the "divine assistance" He gives that helps us become worthy. It is not just a reward for the righteous. It is the "endowment of strength" He gives that helps us become righteous.[27] We are not just walking *toward* God and Christ. We are walking *with* Them.[28]

Across the Church, young people recite the Young Women and Aaronic Priesthood Quorum Themes. From New Zealand to Spain to Ethiopia to Japan, young women say, "I cherish the gift of repentance." From Chile to Guatemala to Moroni, Utah, young men say, "As I strive to serve, exercise faith, repent, and improve each day, I will qualify to receive temple blessings and the enduring joy of the gospel."

I promise those blessings and that joy are real and within reach for those who keep all the commandments *and* "him that seeketh so to do."[29] When you feel like you have failed too many times to keep trying, remember Christ's Atonement and the grace it makes possible are real.[30] "[His] arm of mercy is extended towards you."[31] You are loved—today, in 20 years, and forever. In the name of Jesus Christ, amen.

Notes

1. See John 3:3–6; Mosiah 27:25.
2. See Neal A. Maxwell, "I Will Arise and Go to My Father," *Ensign,* Sept. 1993, 65–68.
3. See Helaman 3:21.
4. See 2 Corinthians 5:17; Mosiah 3:19.
5. Russell M. Nelson, "We Can Do Better and Be Better," *Ensign* or *Liahona,* May 2019, 67.
6. See Mosiah 26:30; Moroni 6:8; Doctrine and Covenants 1:31–32.
7. See Doctrine and Covenants 58:43.
8. Mosiah 5:2.
9. See Jacob 6:11; Alma 15:17.
10. See 2 Nephi 31:20; Mosiah 18:10; Doctrine and Covenants 20:77.
11. See Luke 15:11–32; Romans 3:23–25. Elder Gerrit W. Gong said, "To be worthy does not mean to be perfect" ("Always Remember Him," *Ensign* or *Liahona,* May 2016, 109). Addressing the students at Brigham Young University, President Cecil O. Samuelson explained: "One can be fully worthy in [the] gospel sense and yet still be growing while dealing with personal imperfections. . . . Worthiness is vital, but it is not the same as perfection" ("Be Ye Therefore Perfect" [Brigham Young University devotional, Sept. 6, 2011], 1, 5, speeches.byu.edu). Elder Marvin J. Ashton said: "Worthiness is a process, and perfection is an eternal trek. We can be worthy to enjoy certain privileges without being perfect" ("On Being Worthy," *Ensign, May* 1989, 20).
12. Elder Neil L. Andersen has called for "uncompromising honesty" and taught, "Honesty is the

heart of spirituality and must be at the center of true and lasting repentance" (*The Divine Gift of Forgiveness* [2019], 193, 48).

13. Elder Neil L. Andersen wrote, "We may slip back at times, but let us quickly and humbly return to our knees and move again in the right direction" (*The Divine Gift of Forgiveness*, 208).

14. Bruce C. Hafen, *The Broken Heart* (1989), 186.

15. Doctrine and Covenants 46:9; emphasis added.

16. See Doctrine and Covenants 10:67.

17. Richard G. Scott, "Personal Strength through the Atonement of Jesus Christ," *Ensign* or *Liahona*, Nov. 2013, 83.

18. See Doctrine and Covenants 6:35–37.

19. President Russell M. Nelson said: "The Lord does not expect perfection from us at this point in our eternal progression. But He does expect us to *become increasingly pure*" ("We Can Do Better and Be Better," 68; emphasis added).

20. Mosiah 21:16.

21. D. Todd Christofferson, "Recognizing God's Hand in Our Daily Blessings," *Ensign*, Jan. 2012, 20–21; *Liahona*, Jan. 2012, 28–29; see also D. Todd Christofferson, "The Divine Gift of Repentance," *Ensign* or *Liahona*, Nov. 2011, 38–41.

22. See Joshua 1:5, 9; Isaiah 41:10; Matthew 11:28–30; 2 Nephi 28:32; Doctrine and Covenants 24:8.

23. D. Todd Christofferson, "Free Forever, to Act for Themselves," *Ensign* or *Liahona*, Nov. 2014, 19.

24. Dieter F. Uchtdorf, "Five Messages That All of God's Children Need to Hear" (Brigham Young University devotional, Aug. 17, 2021), 3, speeches.byu.edu.

25. See Ether 1:42–43.

26. 3 Nephi 14:11.

27. Dieter F. Uchtdorf, "The Gift of Grace," *Ensign* or *Liahona*, May 2015, 107; see also 2 Nephi 2:3; Jacob 4:7. President Russell M. Nelson has said, "The Lord does not require *perfect* faith for us to have access to His *perfect* power" ("Christ Is Risen; Faith in Him Will Move Mountains," *Liahona*, May 2021, 102).

28. See Deuteronomy 2:7; Matthew 1:23; Doctrine and Covenants 100:12. Elder Robert E. Wells wrote: "Our Heavenly Father is not an absentee God, nor is Jesus dead. They are relevant today as never before" (*The Mount and the Master* [1991], 26).

29. Doctrine and Covenants 46:9.

30. See Sheri Dew, *Amazed by Grace* (2015), 4.

31. 3 Nephi 9:14.

TO BE A FOLLOWER OF CHRIST

ELDER ALFRED KYUNGU
Of the Seventy

In my personal study of the scriptures, I have been impressed by the conversion of Saul of Tarsus, who later became known as Paul, as described in the Bible.

Paul was an active man in the persecution of the Church and the Christians. But because of the power of heaven and the Atonement of Jesus Christ, he was changed completely, and he became one of the great servants of God. His model of life was the Savior Jesus Christ.

In one of Paul's teachings to the Corinthians, he invited them to be his followers as he himself was a follower of Christ (see 1 Corinthians 11:1). This is a sincere and valid invitation from Paul's time until today: to be a follower of Christ.

I began to reflect on what it means to become a follower of Christ. And more important, I began to ask, "In what way should I imitate Him?"

To be a follower of Christ is to strive to conform our actions, conduct, and lives to those of the Savior. It is to acquire virtues. It is to be a true disciple of Jesus Christ.

I have studied some aspects of the Savior's life, and I have retained, as part of my message today, four of His qualities that I try to imitate and that I share with you.

The first quality of the Savior is humility. Jesus Christ was very humble from the premortal life. At the Council in Heaven, He recognized and allowed the will of God to prevail in the plan of salvation for mankind. He said, "Father, thy will be done, and the glory be thine forever" (Moses 4:2).

We know that Jesus Christ taught humility and humbled Himself to glorify His Father.

Let us live in humility because it brings peace (see Doctrine and Covenants 19:23). Humility precedes glory, and it brings God's favor upon us: "Yea, all of you be subject one to another, and be clothed with humility: for God resisteth the proud, and giveth grace to the humble" (1 Peter 5:5). Humility brings gentle answers. It is the source of a righteous character.

Elder Dale G. Renlund taught:

"Individuals who walk humbly with God remember what Heavenly Father and Jesus Christ have done for them."

"We act honorably with God by walking humbly with Him" ("Do Justly, Love Mercy, and Walk Humbly with God," *Ensign* or *Liahona*, Nov. 2020, 111, 109).

The second quality of the Savior is courage. When I think of Jesus Christ at the age of 12, sitting in the temple of God among the doctors of the law and teaching them divine things, I note that He already had, very early in His life, a good sense of courage, a particular courage. While most would expect to see the young boy being taught by the doctors of the law, He was teaching them as "they were hearing him, and asking him questions" (Joseph Smith Translation, Luke 2:46 [in Luke 2:46, footnote *c*]).

We served a full-time mission in the Democratic Republic of the Congo Mbuji-Mayi Mission from 2016 to 2019. The way to travel in the mission from one zone to another was by road. A phenomenon had arisen in that area with bandits armed with bladed weapons breaking onto the road and disturbing the movement of travelers.

Five missionaries traveling from one zone to another as part of the transfer were victims of these disturbances. Having been victims of this phenomenon ourselves sometimes before, we began to fear for the lives and safety of all of us, even hesitating to travel on these roads to visit the missionaries and hold zone conferences. We did not know how long it was going to last. I drew up a report, which I sent to the Area Presidency, and I expressed my feelings of fear about continuing to travel when the road was the only way to reach our missionaries.

In his reply, Elder Kevin Hamilton, who was our President of the Africa Southeast Area, wrote to me: "My counsel is to do the best you can. Be wise and be prayerful. Do not knowingly put yourselves or your missionaries in harm's way, but at the same time go forward in faith. 'For God hath not given us the spirit of fear; but of power, and of love, and of a sound mind' (2 Timothy 1:7)."

This exhortation greatly strengthened us and allowed us to continue to travel and serve with courage until the end of our mission, because we heard direction from our Father in Heaven through that scripture.

In modern scripture, we read the inspired words of the Prophet Joseph Smith reflecting the Lord's encouragement to us: "Brethren, shall we not go on in so great a cause? Go forward and not backward. Courage, brethren; and on, on to the victory!" (Doctrine and Covenants 128:22).

Let us have the courage to do what is right even when it is unpopular—the courage to defend our faith and to act by faith. Let us have the courage to repent daily, the courage to accept God's will and obey His commandments. Let us have the courage to live righteously and to do what is expected of us in our various responsibilities and positions.

The third quality of the Savior is forgiveness. During His mortal ministry, the Savior prevented a woman who had been taken in adultery from being stoned. He charged her to "go, and sin no more" (John 8:11). This moved her toward repentance and eventual forgiveness, for as the scriptures record, "the woman glorified God from that hour, and believed on his name" (Joseph Smith Translation, John 8:11 [in John 8:11, footnote *c*]).

During a Christmas devotional in December 2018, our dear President Russell M. Nelson spoke about four gifts we have received from the Savior. He said that one gift the Savior offers is the ability to *forgive*:

"Through His infinite Atonement, you can forgive those who have hurt you and who may never accept responsibility for their cruelty to you.

"It is usually easy to forgive one who sincerely and humbly seeks your forgiveness. But the Savior will grant you the ability to forgive anyone who has mistreated you in any way" ("Four Gifts That

Jesus Christ Offers to You" [First Presidency Christmas devotional, Dec. 2, 2018], broadcasts.ChurchofJesusChrist.org).

Let us sincerely forgive each other to obtain the forgiveness of the Father. Forgiveness sets us free and makes us worthy to partake of the sacrament every Sunday. Forgiveness is required for us to be truly disciples of Jesus Christ.

The fourth quality of the Savior is sacrifice. It is part of the gospel of Jesus Christ. The Savior gave the supreme sacrifice of His life for us so that we would be redeemed. Feeling the pain of sacrifice, He asked His Father to keep the cup away, but He went to the end of the eternal sacrifice. This is the Atonement of Jesus Christ.

President M. Russell Ballard taught this: "Sacrifice is [the] demonstration of pure love. The degree of our love for the Lord, for the gospel, and for our fellowman can be measured by what we are willing to sacrifice for them" ("The Blessings of Sacrifice," *Ensign*, May 1992, 76).

We can sacrifice our time to perform ministering, to serve others, to do good, to do family history work, and to magnify our Church calling.

We can give of our financial means by paying tithing, fast offerings, and other donations to build the kingdom of God on earth. We need sacrifice to keep the covenants we have made with the Savior.

My prayer is that by following Jesus Christ and drawing upon the blessings of His Atonement, we become more and more humble, we are more courageous, we forgive more and more, and we sacrifice more for His kingdom.

I testify that our Heavenly Father lives and that He knows each of us individually, that Jesus is the Christ, that President Russell M. Nelson is God's prophet today. I testify that The Church of Jesus Christ of Latter-day Saints is the kingdom of God on earth and the Book of Mormon is true. In the name of Jesus Christ, our Redeemer, amen.

HOLD UP YOUR LIGHT

ELDER MARCUS B. NASH
Of the Seventy

While on a flight to Peru a few years ago, I was seated next to a self-proclaimed atheist. He asked me why I believe in God. In the delightful conversation that ensued, I told him that I believed in God because Joseph Smith saw Him—and then I added that my knowledge of God also came from personal, real spiritual experience. I shared my belief that "all things denote there is a God"[1] and asked him how he believed the earth—this oasis of life in the vacuum of space—came into existence. He replied that, in his words, "the accident" could have happened over eons of time. When I explained how highly improbable it would be for an "accident" to produce such beauty and order, he was quiet for a time and then good-naturedly said, "You got me." I asked if he would read the Book of Mormon. He said he would, so I sent him a copy.

Years later I made a new friend while in an airport in Lagos, Nigeria. We became acquainted as he checked my passport. I asked him about his religious beliefs, and he expressed strong faith in God. I shared the joy and vibrancy of the restored gospel of Jesus Christ and asked if he would like to learn more from the missionaries. He said yes, was taught, and was baptized. A year or two later, as I walked through the airport in Liberia, I heard a voice call out my name. I turned, and that same young man approached with a big smile. We joyfully embraced, and he let me know that he was active in the Church and working with the missionaries to teach his girlfriend.

Now, I do not know whether my atheist friend ever read the Book of Mormon or joined the Church. My second friend did. For both of them, my responsibility[2]—my opportunity—was the same: hold up the gospel light—to love, share, and invite each of them in a normal, natural way.[3]

Brothers and sisters, I have experienced the blessings of sharing the gospel, and they are remarkable. Here are a few of them:

Sharing the Gospel Brings Joy and Hope

You see, you and I know that we lived as children of our Heavenly Father before coming to this earth[4] and that the earth was created for the purpose of giving each person the opportunity to obtain a body, gain experience, learn, and grow in order to receive eternal life—which is God's life.[5] Heavenly Father knew we would suffer and sin on earth, so He sent His Son, whose "matchless life"[6] and infinite atoning sacrifice[7] make it possible for us to be forgiven, healed, and made whole.[8]

To know these truths is life changing! When a person learns the glorious purpose of life, comes to understand that Christ forgives and succors those who follow Him, and then chooses to follow Christ into the waters of baptism, life changes for the better—even when the external circumstances of life do not.

A radiantly happy sister I met in Onitsha, Nigeria, told me that from the time she learned the gospel and was baptized (and now I use her words), "everything is good for me. I am happy. I am in heaven."[9] Sharing the gospel kindles joy and hope in the souls of both giver and receiver. Truly, "how great shall be your joy"[10] as you share the gospel! Sharing the gospel is joy upon joy, hope upon hope.[11]

Sharing the Gospel Brings God's Power into Our Lives

When we were baptized, each of us entered into a perpetual[12] covenant with God to "serve him and keep his commandments,"[13] which includes "to stand as witnesses of [Him] at all times and in all things, and in all places."[14] As we "abide in" Him by keeping this covenant, the enlivening, sustaining, sanctifying power of godliness flows into our lives from Christ, just as a branch receives nourishment from the vine.[15]

Sharing the Gospel Protects Us from Temptation

The Lord commands:

"Hold up your light that it may shine unto the world. Behold

I am the light which ye shall hold up—that which ye have seen me do. . . .

". . . I have commanded that . . . ye should come unto me, that ye might feel and see; even so shall ye do unto the world; and whosoever breaketh this commandment suffereth himself to be led into temptation."[16]

Choosing to not hold up the gospel light moves us to the shadows, where we are susceptible to temptation. Importantly, the converse is true: choosing to hold up the gospel light brings us more fully into that light and the protection it provides against temptation. What a tremendous blessing in today's world!

Sharing the Gospel Brings Healing

Sister Tiffany Myloan accepted the invitation to support the missionaries despite very heavy personal struggles, including questions about her faith. She recently told me that supporting the missionaries has renewed her faith and sense of well-being. In her words, "Missionary work is so healing."[17]

Joy. Hope. Sustaining power from God. Protection from temptation. Healing. All of these—and more (including forgiveness of sins)[18]—distill upon us from heaven as we share the gospel.

Now, Turning to Our Great Opportunity

Brothers and sisters, "there are many . . . among all . . . parties, [sects,] and denominations . . . who are only kept from the truth because they know not where to find it."[19] The need to hold up our light has never been greater in all human history. And the truth has never been more accessible.

Jimmy Ton, who grew up Buddhist, was impressed by a family who shared their life on YouTube. When he learned that they were members of The Church of Jesus Christ of Latter-day Saints, he studied the gospel online by himself, read the Book of Mormon using the app, and was baptized after meeting with the missionaries in college.[20] Elder Ton is now a full-time missionary himself.

He and his fellow missionaries around the world are the Lord's battalion—to quote our prophet.[21] These missionaries buck the trend of the world: while surveys report that Gen Z is turning *away* from God,[22] our stripling warrior[23] elders and sisters are turning people *to* God. And increasing numbers of members of the Church are uniting with the missionaries in sharing the gospel, helping more and more friends to come unto Christ and His Church.

Our Latter-day Saints in Liberia helped 507 friends enter the waters of baptism during the 10 months there were no full-time missionaries serving in their country. When one of our wonderful stake presidents there heard that the full-time missionaries may be returning, he remarked, "Oh good, now they can help us with *our* work."

He is correct: the gathering of Israel—the greatest cause on this earth[24]—is *our* covenant responsibility. And this is *our* time! My invitation today is simple: share the gospel. Be you and hold up the light. Pray for heaven's help and follow spiritual promptings. Share your life normally and naturally; invite another person to come and see, to come and help, and to come and belong.[25] And then rejoice as you and those you love receive the promised blessings.

I know that in Christ these good tidings are preached to the meek; in Christ are the brokenhearted bound up; in Christ is liberty proclaimed to the captives; and in Christ, only in Christ, are those who mourn given beauty for ashes.[26] Hence, the great need to make these things known![27]

I testify that Jesus Christ is the author and the finisher of our faith.[28] He will finish, He will complete, our exercise of faith—however imperfect—in holding up the gospel light. He will work miracles in our lives and in the lives of all He gathers, for He is a God of miracles.[29] In the wondrous name of Jesus Christ, amen.

Notes

1. Alma 30:44.
2. See Ether 12:36–37.
3. See *General Handbook: Serving in The Church of Jesus Christ of Latter-day Saints*, chapter 23, to learn doctrine and principles and to view videos showing examples of ways to hold up the light and share the gospel.
4. See "The Family: A Proclamation to the World," ChurchofJesusChrist.org; see also Job 38:4–7; Acts 17:29; Romans 8:16–17; Hebrews 12:9; Abraham 3:18–25.

5. See Alma 12:30; Doctrine and Covenants 14:7; Moses 1:39; Abraham 3:22–25.
6. "The Living Christ: The Testimony of the Apostles," ChurchofJesusChrist.org.
7. See 2 Nephi 9:7.
8. See Luke 22:39–46; 1 Nephi 15:34; Alma 7:11–12; Abraham 3:27.
9. Video interview, Nov. 23, 2019.
10. See Doctrine and Covenants 18:10–16; see also Alma 36:24–28.
11. See Alma 26:11, 13, 35; Doctrine and Covenants 18:10–16.
12. See Jeremiah 50:4–6.
13. Mosiah 18:10.
14. Mosiah 18:9; see also verses 8–13.
15. See John 15:4–5.
16. 3 Nephi 18:24–25.
17. Personal correspondence.
18. See Doctrine and Covenants 62:3.
19. Doctrine and Covenants 123:12; see also 1 Corinthians 14:8.
20. Personal correspondence.
21. See Russell M. Nelson, "Hope of Israel" (worldwide youth devotional, June 3, 2018), HopeofIsrael.ChurchofJesusChrist.org.
22. See "Atheism Doubles among Generation Z," Barna Group research release, Jan. 24, 2018, barna.com.
23. See Alma 53:20–21; 56:46–47; 57:19–27.
24. See Russell M. Nelson, "Hope of Israel."
25. See share.ChurchofJesusChrist.org for apostolic teaching and video examples showing what fellow Saints across the world are doing to love, share, and invite other individuals to enjoy the blessings of the Church and gospel of Jesus Christ.
26. See Isaiah 61:1–3.
27. See 2 Nephi 2:8.
28. See Moroni 6:4.
29. See Mormon 9:18–21.

THE FAITH TO ASK AND THEN TO ACT

PRESIDENT HENRY B. EYRING
Second Counselor in the First Presidency

My beloved brothers and sisters, I am grateful for the opportunity to speak with you in this Saturday evening session of general conference. In his introduction to the conference this morning, President Russell M. Nelson said that "pure revelation for the questions in your heart will make this conference rewarding and unforgettable. If you have not yet sought for the ministering of the Holy Ghost to help you hear what the Lord would have you hear during these two days, I invite you to do so now."[1] I have sought for that blessing as I have prepared to receive revelation for this visit with you. My earnest prayer is that you may receive revelation from God.

The way to receive revelation from God has not changed from the days of Adam and Eve. It has been the same for all called servants of the Lord from the beginning to the present day. It is the same for you and me. It is always done by exercising faith.[2]

The teenage Joseph Smith had faith sufficient to ask a question of God, believing that God would answer his heartfelt need. The answer that came changed the world. He wanted to know what church to join to be cleansed of sin. The answer he received encouraged him to keep asking ever-better questions and to act on the continuing flow of revelation that had just begun.[3]

Your experience can possibly be similar in this conference. You have questions for which you seek answers. You have at least enough faith to hope that you will receive answers from the Lord through His servants.[4] You will not have the opportunity to ask aloud for answers from the speakers, but you can ask your loving Father in prayer.

I know from experience that answers will come to fit your needs and your spiritual preparation. If you need an answer that is important to your eternal welfare or that of others, the answer is more likely to come. Yet even then, you may receive—as did Joseph Smith—the answer to be patient.[5]

If your faith in Jesus Christ has led to a heart softened through the effects of His Atonement, you will be more able to feel the whisperings of the Spirit in answer to your prayers. My personal experience is that the still, small voice—which is real—is clear and discernible in my mind when I feel an internal quiet and submission to the Lord's will. That feeling of humility can be best described as "Not my will, but thine, be done."[6]

This process of revelation is why you will hear speakers teach in this conference what is called the doctrine of Christ.[7] Revelation comes to us in proportion to the degree to which we have sought to take the doctrine of Christ into our hearts and implement it in our lives.

You remember from the Book of Mormon that Nephi taught us that faith in Jesus Christ is the key to receiving revelations of truth and the key to having the confidence that we are following the Savior's direction. Nephi wrote the following words centuries before the birth of Jesus Christ into mortality:

"Angels speak by the power of the Holy Ghost; wherefore, they speak the words of Christ. Wherefore, I said unto you, feast upon the words of Christ; for behold, the words of Christ will tell you all things what ye should do.

"Wherefore, now after I have spoken these words, if ye cannot understand them it will be because ye ask not, neither do ye knock; wherefore, ye are not brought into the light, but must perish in the dark.

"For behold, again I say unto you that if ye will enter in by the way, and receive the Holy Ghost, it will show unto you all things what ye should do.

"Behold, this is the doctrine of Christ, and there will be no more doctrine given until after he shall manifest himself unto you in the flesh. And when he shall manifest himself unto you in the flesh, the things which he shall say unto you shall ye observe to do."[8]

The Lord will say things through His servants to you and to me today and in the days ahead. He will tell us what things we should do.[9] The Savior will not shout commands to you and me. As He taught Elijah:

"And he said, Go forth, and stand upon the mount before the Lord. And, behold, the Lord passed by, and a great and strong wind rent the mountains, and brake in pieces the rocks before the Lord; but the Lord was not in the wind: and after the wind an earthquake; but the Lord was not in the earthquake:

"And after the earthquake a fire; but the Lord was not in the fire: and after the fire a still small voice."[10]

Hearing that voice will come from our faith in Him. With sufficient faith, we will ask for direction with the intent to go and do whatever He asks.[11] We will have developed the faith to know that whatever He asks will bless others and that we can be purified in the process because of His love for us.

As our faith in Jesus Christ will have led us to ask the Father for answers, that faith will also have brought the Savior's softening touch enough for us to hear His direction and be determined and excited to obey. We then will sing the words of the hymn with joy, even when the work is hard: "Sweet is the work, my God, my King."[12]

The more we have the doctrine of Christ in our lives and hearts, the more we feel greater love and sympathy for those who have never had the blessings of faith in Jesus Christ or are struggling to maintain it. It is hard to keep the Lord's commandments without faith and trust in Him. As some lose their faith in the Savior, they may even attack His counsel, calling good evil and evil good.[13] To avoid this tragic error, it is crucial that any personal revelation we receive be consonant with the teachings of the Lord and His prophets.

Brothers and sisters, it takes faith to be obedient to the Lord's commandments. It takes faith in Jesus Christ to serve others for Him. It takes faith to go out to teach His gospel and offer it to people who may not feel the voice of the Spirit or may even deny the reality of the message. But as we exercise our faith in Christ—and follow His living prophet—faith will increase across the world. Because of technology, perhaps more of God's children will hear and recognize the word of God this weekend than during any other two days in history.

With increasing faith that this is the Lord's Church and kingdom on earth, more members pay tithing and donate to assist those in need, even as those members face trials of their own. With faith that they are called by Jesus Christ, missionaries across the world have found ways to rise above the challenges created by a pandemic, doing so with courage and good cheer. And in their extra effort, their faith has grown stronger.

Opposition and trials have long been a seedbed for the growth of faith. That has always been true, especially since the beginning of the Restoration and the founding of the Lord's Church.[14]

What President George Q. Cannon said long ago is true today and will be until the Savior comes personally to lead His Church and His people: "Obedience to the Gospel brings [people] into very close and intimate relationship with the Lord. It establishes a close connection between men on the earth and our Great Creator in the heavens. It brings to the human mind a feeling of perfect confidence in the Almighty and in His willingness to listen to and answer the supplications of those who trust in Him. In times of trial and difficulty this confidence is beyond price. Trouble may come upon the individual or upon the people, disaster may threaten and every human hope may seem to be overthrown, yet, where [people] have availed themselves of the privileges which obedience to the Gospel brings, they have a sure standing place; their feet are upon a rock that cannot be moved."[15]

It is my testimony that the rock upon which we stand is our witness that Jesus is the Christ; that this is His Church, which He leads personally; and that President Russell M. Nelson is His living prophet today.

President Nelson seeks and receives direction from the Lord. He is for me an example of seeking that direction with the determination to follow it. That same determination to be obedient to the Lord's direction is in the hearts of all those who have spoken or will speak, pray, or sing in this general conference of His Church.

I pray that those across the earth who watch or listen to this conference will have the feeling of the Lord's love for them. Heavenly Father has answered my prayer that I might feel at least a tiny part of the Savior's love for you and His love for His Heavenly Father, who is our Heavenly Father.

I testify that Jesus Christ lives. He is our Savior and our Redeemer. This is His Church. He is at its head. He, with His Heavenly Father, appeared in person to Joseph Smith in a grove of trees in New York. The gospel of Jesus Christ and His priesthood were restored through heavenly messengers.[16] By the power of the Holy Ghost, I know that is true.

I pray that you may have that same witness. I pray that you will ask Heavenly Father for the faith in Jesus Christ you need to make and keep the covenants that will allow the Holy Ghost to be your constant companion. I leave you with my love and my sure witness in the sacred name of Jesus Christ, amen.

Notes

1. Russell M. Nelson, "Pure Truth, Pure Doctrine, and Pure Revelation," *Liahona*, Nov. 2021, 6.
2. See Matthew 7:7–8; Alma 32:26–43.
3. See Joseph Smith—History 1:13–26.
4. See Hebrews 11:1; Alma 32:21.
5. See Joseph Smith—History 1:53; see also Doctrine and Covenants 24:8; 121:1–8.
6. Luke 22:42.
7. See 2 Nephi 31; 3 Nephi 11:31–39.
8. 2 Nephi 32:3–6.
9. See Doctrine and Covenants 1:38.
10. 1 Kings 19:11–12; see also Doctrine and Covenants 85:6.
11. See 1 Nephi 3:7; 4:6.
12. "Sweet Is the Work," *Hymns*, no. 147.
13. See Isaiah 5:20; Moroni 7:12–19.
14. See 2 Nephi 2:1–2, 11.
15. *Gospel Truth: Discourses and Writings of George Q. Cannon*, sel. Jerreld L. Newquist (1987), 116.
16. See Joseph Smith—History 1:17, 30–42, 68–72; see also Doctrine and Covenants 27:12–13; 110.

SUNDAY MORNING SESSION

OCTOBER 3, 2021

DAILY RESTORATION

ELDER DIETER F. UCHTDORF
Of the Quorum of the Twelve Apostles

We gather this beautiful Sabbath morning to speak of Christ, rejoice in His gospel, and support and sustain one another as we walk in "the way" of our Savior.[1]

As members of The Church of Jesus Christ of Latter-day Saints, we assemble for this purpose every Sabbath day throughout the year. If you are not a member of the Church, we welcome you most warmly and thank you for joining with us to worship the Savior and learn of Him. Like you, we are striving—though imperfectly—to become better friends, neighbors, and human beings,[2] and we seek to do this by following our Exemplar, Jesus Christ.

We hope you can feel the sincerity of our testimony. Jesus Christ lives! He is the Son of the living God, and He directs prophets on the earth in our day. We invite all to come, hear the word of God, and partake of His goodness! I bear my personal witness that God is among us and that He will surely draw near to all who draw near to Him.[3]

We consider it an honor to walk with you in the Master's strait and narrow path of discipleship.

The Art of Walking in a Straight Line

There is an oft-repeated theory that people who are lost walk in circles. Not long ago, scientists at the Max Planck Institute for Biological Cybernetics tested that theory. They took participants to a thick forest and gave them simple instructions: "Walk in a straight line." There were no visible landmarks. The test subjects had to rely solely on their sense of direction.

How do you think they did?

The scientists concluded, "People really [do] walk in circles when they do not have reliable cues to their walking direction."[4] When questioned afterwards, some participants self-confidently claimed that they had not deviated in the slightest. Despite their high confidence, GPS data showed that they walked in loops as tight as 20 meters in diameter.

Why do we do have such a hard time walking in a straight line? Some researchers hypothesize that small, seemingly insignificant deviations in terrain make the difference. Others have pointed to the fact that we all have one leg that is slightly stronger than the other. "More likely," however, we struggle to walk straight ahead "[because] of increasing uncertainty about where straight ahead is."[5]

Whatever the cause, it is human nature: without reliable landmarks, we drift off course.

Straying from the Path

Isn't it interesting how small, seemingly insignificant factors can make a major difference in our lives?

I know this from personal experience as a pilot. Every time I started the approach to an airport, I knew that much of my remaining work would consist of making constant minor course corrections to safely direct the aircraft to our desired landing runway.

You might have a similar experience when driving a vehicle. Wind, road irregularities, imperfect wheel alignment, inattentiveness—not to mention the actions of other drivers—all can push you off your intended path. Fail to pay attention to these factors and you may end up having a bad day.[6]

This applies to us physically.

It also applies to us spiritually.

Most of the changes in our spiritual lives—both positive and negative—happen gradually, a step at a time. Like the participants in the Max Planck study, we may not realize when we veer off course. We may even have high confidence that we are walking a straight line. But the fact is that without the help of landmarks to guide us, we inevitably deviate off course and end up in places we never thought we would be.

This is true for individuals. It is also true for societies and nations. The scriptures are filled with examples.

The book of Judges records that after Joshua died, "there arose another generation . . . which knew not the Lord, nor yet the works which he had done for Israel."[7]

Despite the astonishing heavenly interventions, visitations, rescues, and miraculous victories the children of Israel witnessed during the lifetimes of Moses and Joshua, within a generation the people had abandoned the Way and began walking according to their own desires. And, of course, it did not take long before they paid the price for that behavior.

Sometimes this falling away takes generations. Sometimes it happens in a matter of years or even months.[8] But we are all susceptible. No matter how strong our spiritual experiences have been in the past, as human beings we tend to wander. That has been the pattern from the days of Adam until now.

Here's the Good News

But all is not lost. Unlike the wandering test subjects, we have reliable, visible landmarks that we can use to evaluate our course.

And what are these landmarks?

Surely they include daily prayer and pondering the scriptures and using inspired tools like *Come, Follow Me*. Each day, we can approach the throne of God in humility and honesty. We can ponder our actions and review the moments of our day—considering our will and desires in light of His. If we have drifted, we plead with God to restore us, and we commit to do better.

This time of introspection is an opportunity for recalibration. It is a garden of reflection where we can walk with the Lord and be instructed, edified, and purified by the written and Spirit-revealed word of our Heavenly Father. It is a sacred time when we remember our solemn covenants to follow the gentle Christ, when we assess our progress and align ourselves with the spiritual landmarks God has provided for His children.

Think of it as your personal, *daily restoration*. On our journey as pilgrims on the path of glory, we know how easy it is to fall away. But just as minor deviations can draw us out of the Savior's Way, so too can small and simple acts of realignment assuredly lead us back.

When darkness creeps into our lives, as it often does, our daily restoration opens our hearts to heavenly light, which illuminates our souls, chasing away shadows, fears, and doubts.

Small Rudders, Large Ships

If we seek it, surely "God shall give unto [us] knowledge by his Holy Spirit, yea, by the unspeakable gift of the Holy Ghost."[9] As often as we ask, He will teach us the Way and help us follow it.

This, of course, takes a steady effort on our part. We cannot be content with spiritual experiences of the past. We need a steady flow.

We can't rely on others' testimonies forever. We must build our own.

We need an ongoing, daily infusion of heavenly light.

We need "times of refreshing."[10] Times of personal restoration.

"Rolling waters" cannot long "remain impure."[11] To keep our thoughts and actions pure, we have to keep rolling!

After all, the Restoration of the gospel and the Church is not something that happened once and is over. It is an *ongoing process*— one day at a time, one heart at a time.

As our days go, so go our lives. One author put it this way: "A day is like a whole life. You start out doing one thing, but end up doing something else, plan to run an errand, but never get there. . . . And at the end of your life, your whole existence has that same haphazard quality, too. Your whole life has the same shape as a single day."[12]

Do you want to change the shape of your life?

Change the shape of your day.

Do you want to change your day?

Change this hour.

Change what you think, feel, and do at this very moment.

A small rudder can steer a large ship.[13]

Small bricks can become magnificent mansions.

Small seeds can become towering sequoias.

Minutes and hours well spent are the building blocks of a life well lived. They can inspire goodness, lift us from the captivity of

123

imperfections, and lead us upward to the redemptive path of forgiveness and sanctification.

The God of New Beginnings

With you, I lift my heart in gratitude for the magnificent gift of new opportunity, new life, new hope.

We lift our voices in praise of our bountiful and forgiving God. For surely He is a God of new beginnings. The sublime end of all His labor is to help us, His children, succeed in our quest for immortality and eternal life.[14]

We can become new creatures in Christ, for God has promised, "As often as my people repent will I forgive them their trespasses against me"[15] and "remember them no more."[16]

My beloved brothers and sisters, dear friends, we all drift from time to time.

But we can get back on course. We can navigate our way through the darkness and trials of this life and find our way back to our loving Heavenly Father if we seek and accept the spiritual landmarks He has provided, embrace personal revelation, and strive for *daily restoration*. This is how we become true disciples of our beloved Savior, Jesus Christ.

As we do so, God will smile upon us. "The Lord shall . . . bless thee in the land which the Lord thy God giveth thee. The Lord shall establish thee an holy people unto himself."[17]

That we will seek daily restoration and continually strive to walk in the Way of Jesus Christ is my prayer. In the name of Jesus Christ, amen.

Notes

1. Jesus taught, "I am the way, the truth, and the life" (John 14:6). The *NIV First-Century Study Bible* contains this explanation: "The image of a path or way in the Hebrew Bible often stood for keeping the commandments or teachings of God [see Psalm 1:1; 16:11; 86:11]. This was a common ancient metaphor for active participation in a set of beliefs, teachings or practices. The Dead Sea Scrolls community called themselves followers of 'the way,' by which they meant they were followers of their own interpretation of the path that pleased God. Paul and the first Christians also called themselves 'follower[s] of the Way' [see Acts 24:14]" (in "What the Bible Says about the Way, the Truth, and the Life," Bible Gateway, biblegateway.com/topics/the-way-the-truth-and-the-life).

   In 1873, an ancient book titled the *Didache* was discovered in the library of the patriarch of Jerusalem at Constantinople. Many scholars believe it was written and used in the late first century (AD 80–100). The *Didache* begins with these words: "Two ways there are, one of life and one of death, but there is a great difference between the two ways. The way of life, then, is this: First, thou shalt love the God who made thee; secondly, thy neighbor as thyself" (*Teaching of the Twelve Apostles*, trans. Roswell D. Hitchcock and Francis Brown [1884], 3).

Other sources, such as *The Expositor's Bible Commentary*, point out that "during the early existence of the church, those who accepted Jesus' messiahship and claimed him as their Lord called themselves those of 'the Way' [see Acts 19:9, 23; 22:4; 24:14, 22]" (ed. Frank E. Gaebelein and others [1981], 9:370).

2. See Mosiah 2:17.
3. See Doctrine and Covenants 88:63.
4. "Walking in Circles," Aug. 20, 2009, Max-Planck-Gesellschaft, mpg.de.
5. "Walking in Circles," mpg.de. This image shows the GPS tracking of four participants in the study. Three of them walked on a cloudy day. One of them (SM) started walking while the sun was covered by clouds, but after 15 minutes the clouds dissipated, and the participant could see glimpses of sun. Notice how, once the sun was visible, the walker was much more successful in walking a straight line.
6. For one tragic example of how a course error of a mere two degrees caused a passenger jet to crash into Mount Erebus in Antarctica, killing 257 people, see Dieter F. Uchtdorf, "A Matter of a Few Degrees," *Ensign* or *Liahona*, May 2008, 57–60.
7. Judges 2:10.
8. After Christ's visit to the Americas, the people truly repented of their sins, were baptized, and received the Holy Ghost. Where they were once a contentious and prideful people, now "there were no contentions and disputations among them, and every man did deal justly one with another" (4 Nephi 1:2). This period of righteousness lasted some two centuries before pride began to cause people to turn from the Way. However, spiritual drift can also happen much more quickly. As an example, decades earlier, in the 50th year of the reign of the judges in the Book of Mormon, there was "continual peace and great joy" among the people. But because of pride that entered the hearts of Church members, after a short period of four years "there were many dissensions in the church, and there was also a contention among the people, insomuch that there was much bloodshed" (see Helaman 3:32–4:1).
9. Doctrine and Covenants 121:26.
10. Acts 3:19.
11. Doctrine and Covenants 121:33.
12. Michael Crichton, *Jurassic Park* (2015), 190.
13. "Take ships as an example. Although they are so large and are driven by strong winds, they are steered by a very small rudder wherever the pilot wants to go" (James 3:4, New International Version).
14. See Moses 1:39.
15. Mosiah 26:30.
16. Doctrine and Covenants 58:42.
17. Deuteronomy 28:8–9; see also verses 1–7.

INVITE CHRIST TO AUTHOR YOUR STORY

CAMILLE N. JOHNSON
Primary General President

I begin by posing several questions, meant for self-reflection:

- What kind of personal narrative are you writing for your life?
- Is the path you describe in your story straight?
- Does your story end where it began, at your heavenly home?
- Is there an exemplar in your story—and is it the Savior Jesus Christ?

I testify that the Savior is "the author and finisher of our faith."[1] Will you invite Him to be the author and finisher of your story?

He knows the beginning from the end. He was the Creator of heaven and earth. He wants us to return home to Him and our Heavenly Father. He has everything invested in us and wants us to succeed.

What do you suppose keeps us from turning our stories over to Him?

Perhaps this illustration will help your self-assessment.

An effective trial lawyer knows that on cross-examination, you should rarely ask a witness a question to which you do not know the answer. Asking such a question is inviting the witness to tell you—and the judge and jury—something you don't already know. You might get an answer that surprises you and is contrary to the narrative you have developed for your case.

Although asking a witness a question to which you do not know the answer is generally unwise for a trial lawyer, the opposite is true for us. We can ask questions of our loving Heavenly Father, in the name of our merciful Savior, and the witness who answers our questions is the Holy Ghost, who always testifies of truth.[2] Because the Holy Ghost works in perfect unity with Heavenly Father and Jesus Christ, we know that the manifestations of the Holy Ghost are reliable. Why, then, are we sometimes resistant to asking for this kind of heavenly help, truth manifest to us by the Holy Ghost? Why do we put off asking a question to which we do not know the answer when the witness not only is friendly but will always tell the truth?

Perhaps it is because we don't have the faith to accept the answer we might receive. Perhaps it is because the natural man or woman in us is resistant to turning things *completely* over to the Lord and trusting Him *entirely*. Maybe that is why we choose to stick with the narrative we have written for ourselves, a comfortable version of our story unedited by the Master Author. We don't want to ask a question and get an answer that doesn't fit neatly into the story we are writing for ourselves.

Frankly, few of us would probably write into our stories the trials that refine us. But don't we love the glorious culmination of a story we read when the protagonist overcomes the struggle? Trials are the elements of the plot that make our favorite stories compelling, timeless, faith promoting, and worthy of telling. The beautiful struggles written into *our* stories are what draw us closer to the Savior and refine us, making us more like Him.

For David to overcome Goliath, the boy had to take on the giant. The comfortable narrative for David would have been a return to tending sheep. But instead he reflected upon his experience saving lambs from a lion and a bear. And building on those heroic feats, he mustered the faith and courage to let God write his story, declaring, "The Lord that delivered me out of the paw of the lion, and out of the paw of the bear, he will deliver me out of the hand of this Philistine."[3] With a desire to let God prevail, with an ear to the Holy Ghost and a willingness to let the Savior be the author and finisher of his story, the boy David defeated Goliath and saved his people.

The sublime principle of agency does, of course, allow us to write our *own* stories—David could have gone home, back to tending sheep. But Jesus Christ stands ready to use us as divine instruments, sharpened pencils in His hand, to write a masterpiece! He is mercifully willing to use me, a scrawny pencil, as an instrument in His hands, if I have the faith to let Him, if I will let Him author my story.

127

Esther is another beautiful example of letting God prevail. Rather than sticking with a cautious narrative of self-preservation, she exercised faith, turning herself completely over to the Lord. Haman was plotting the destruction of all the Jews in Persia. Mordecai, Esther's relative, became aware of the plot and wrote to her, urging her to talk with the king on behalf of her people. She recounted to him that one who approaches the king without being summoned was subject to death. But in a tremendous act of faith, she asked Mordecai to gather the Jews and fast for her. "I also and my maidens will fast likewise," she said, "and so will I go in unto the king, which is not according to the law: and if I perish, I perish."[4]

Esther was willing to let the Savior write her story even though, through the lens of mortality, the ending may have been tragic. Blessedly, the king received Esther, and the Jews in Persia were saved.

Of course, Esther's level of courage is rarely asked of us. But letting God prevail, letting Him be the author and finisher of our stories, does require us to keep His commandments and the covenants we have made. It is our commandment and covenant keeping that will open the line of communication for us to receive revelation through the Holy Ghost. And it is through the manifestations of the Spirit that we will feel the Master's hand writing our stories with us.

In April 2021, our prophet, President Russell M. Nelson, asked us to consider what we could do if we had more faith in Jesus Christ. With more faith in Jesus Christ, we could ask a question to which we do not know the answer—ask our Father in Heaven, in the name of Jesus Christ, to send an answer through the Holy Ghost, who testifies of truth. If we had more faith, we would ask the question and then be willing to accept the answer we receive, even if it doesn't fit our comfortable narrative. And the promised blessing that will come from acting in faith in Jesus Christ is an increase in faith in Him as our author and finisher. President Nelson declared that we "*receive more* faith by doing something that *requires more* faith."[5]

So, a childless couple suffering with infertility may ask in faith whether they should adopt children and be willing to accept the answer, even though the narrative they had written for themselves included a miraculous birth.

A senior couple may ask whether it is time for them to serve a mission and be willing to go, even though the narrative they had written for themselves included more time in the workforce. Or maybe the answer will be "not yet," and they will learn in later chapters of their story why they were needed at home a little bit longer.

A teenaged young man or young woman may ask in faith whether a pursuit of sports or academics or music is of most value and be willing to follow the promptings of the perfect witness, the Holy Ghost.

Why do we want the Savior to be the author and the finisher of our stories? Because He knows our potential perfectly, He will take us to places we never imagined ourselves. He may make us a David or an Esther. He will stretch us and refine us to be more like Him. The things we will achieve as we act with more faith will increase our faith in Jesus Christ.

Brothers and sisters, just one year ago our dear prophet asked: "Are *you* willing to let God prevail in your life? . . . Are you *willing* to let whatever He needs you to do take precedence over every other ambition?"[6] I humbly add to those prophetic inquiries: "Will you let God be the author and finisher of your story?"

In Revelation we learn that we will stand before God and be judged out of the books of life, according to our works.[7]

We will be judged by our book of life. We can choose to write a comfortable narrative for ourselves. Or we can allow the Master Author and Finisher to write our story with us, letting the role He needs us to play take precedence over other ambitions.

Let Christ be the author and finisher of your story!

Let the Holy Ghost be your witness!

Write a story in which the path you are on is straight, on a course leading you back to your heavenly home to live in the presence of God.

Let the adversity and affliction that are part of every good story be a means by which you draw closer to, and become more like, Jesus Christ.

Tell a story in which you recognize the heavens are open. Ask questions to which you do not know the answer, knowing God is willing to make known His will for you through the Holy Ghost.

Let your narrative be one of faith, following your Exemplar, the Savior Jesus Christ. In the name of Jesus Christ, amen.

Notes

1. Hebrews 12:2; see also Moroni 6:4.
2. See John 14:16–17; Jacob 4:13.
3. 1 Samuel 17:37.
4. Esther 4:16.
5. Russell M. Nelson, "Christ Is Risen; Faith in Him Will Move Mountains," *Liahona*, May 2021, 103.
6. Russell M. Nelson, "Let God Prevail," *Ensign* or *Liahona*, Nov. 2020, 94.
7. See Revelation 20:12.

THE PEACE OF CHRIST ABOLISHES ENMITY

ELDER DALE G. RENLUND
Of the Quorum of the Twelve Apostles

My dear brothers and sisters, during an exercise stress test, the heart's workload is increased. Hearts that can handle walking may struggle to support the demands of running uphill. In this way, the stress test can reveal underlying disease that is not otherwise apparent. Any issues identified can then be treated before they cause serious problems in daily life.

The COVID-19 pandemic has certainly been a global stress test! The test has shown mixed results. Safe and effective vaccines have been developed.[1] Medical professionals, teachers, caregivers, and others have sacrificed heroically—and continue to do so. Many people have displayed generosity and kindness—and continue to do so. Yet, underlying disadvantages have been manifest. Vulnerable individuals have suffered—and continue to do so. Those who work to address these underlying inequalities are to be encouraged and thanked.

The pandemic is also a spiritual stress test for the Savior's Church and its members. The results are likewise mixed. Our lives have been blessed by ministering in a "higher and holier way,"[2] the *Come, Follow Me* curriculum, and home-centered, Church-supported gospel learning. Many have provided compassionate help and comfort during these difficult times and continue to do so.[3]

Yet, in some instances, the spiritual stress test has shown tendencies toward contention and divisiveness. This suggests that we have work to do to change our hearts and to become unified as the Savior's true disciples. This is not a new challenge, but it is a critical one.[4]

When the Savior visited the Nephites, He taught, "There shall be no disputations among you. . . . He that hath the spirit of contention is not of me, but is of the devil, who is the father of contention, and he stirreth up the hearts of men to contend with anger, one with another."[5] When we contend with each other in anger, Satan laughs and the God of heaven weeps.[6]

Satan laughs and God weeps for at least two reasons. First, contention weakens our collective witness to the world of Jesus Christ and the redemption that comes through His "merits, . . . mercy, and grace."[7] The Savior said: "A new commandment I give unto you, That ye love one another. . . . By this shall all men know that ye are my disciples, if ye have love one to another."[8] The converse is also true—everyone knows that we are not His disciples when we do not show love one to another. His latter-day work is compromised when contention or enmity[9] exists among His disciples.[10] Second, contention is spiritually unhealthy for us as individuals. We are robbed of peace, joy, and rest, and our ability to feel the Spirit is compromised.

Jesus Christ explained that His doctrine was not "to stir up the hearts of men with anger, one against another; but [that His] doctrine [is] that such things should be done away."[11] If I am quick to take offense or respond to differences of opinion by becoming angry or judgmental, I "fail" the spiritual stress test. This failed test does not mean that I am hopeless. Rather, it points out that I need to change. And that is good to know.

After the Savior's visit to the Americas, the people were unified; "there was no contention in all the land."[12] Do you think that the people were unified because they were all the same, or because they had no differences of opinion? I doubt it. Instead, contention and enmity disappeared because they placed their discipleship of the Savior above all else. Their differences paled in comparison to their shared love of the Savior, and they were united as "heirs to the kingdom of God."[13] The result was that "there could not be a happier people . . . who had been created by the hand of God."[14]

Unity requires effort.[15] It develops when we cultivate the love of God in our hearts[16] and we focus on our eternal destiny.[17] We are united by our common, primary identity as children of God[18] and our commitment to the truths of the restored gospel. In turn, our love of God and our discipleship of Jesus Christ generate genuine concern for others. We value the kaleidoscope of others' characteristics, perspectives, and talents.[19] If we are unable to place our discipleship to Jesus Christ above personal interests and viewpoints, we should reexamine our priorities and change.

We might be inclined to say, "Of course we can have unity—if only you would agree with me!" A better approach is to ask, "What can I do to foster unity? How can I respond to help this person draw closer to Christ? What can I do to lessen contention and to build a compassionate and caring Church community?"

When love of Christ envelops our lives,[20] we approach disagreements with meekness, patience, and kindness.[21] We worry less about our own sensitivities and more about our neighbor's. We "seek to moderate and unify."[22] We do not engage in "doubtful disputations," judge those with whom we disagree, or try to cause them to stumble.[23] Instead, we assume that those with whom we disagree are doing the best they can with the life experiences they have.

My wife practiced law for over 20 years. As an attorney, she often worked with others who explicitly advocated opposing views. But she learned to disagree without being rude or angry. She might say to opposing counsel, "I can see we are not going to agree on this issue. I like you. I respect your opinion. I hope you can offer me the same courtesy." Often this allowed for mutual respect and even friendship despite differences.

Even former enemies can become united in their discipleship of the Savior.[24] In 2006, I attended the dedication of the Helsinki Finland Temple to honor my father and grandparents, who had been early converts to the Church in Finland. Finns, including my father, had dreamed of a temple in Finland for decades. At the time, the temple district would encompass Finland, Estonia, Latvia, Lithuania, Belarus, and Russia.

At the dedication, I learned something surprising. The first day of general operation had been set aside for Russian members to perform temple ordinances. It is difficult to explain just how astonishing this was. Russia and Finland had fought many wars over the centuries. My father distrusted and disliked not only Russia but all Russians. He had expressed such feelings passionately, and his feelings were typical of Finnish enmity toward Russia. He had memorized epic poems that chronicled 19th-century warfare between Finns and Russians. His experiences during World War II, when Finland and Russia were again antagonists, did nothing to change his opinions.

A year before the dedication of the Helsinki Finland Temple, the temple committee, consisting exclusively of Finnish members, met to discuss plans for the dedication. During the meeting, someone observed that Russian Saints would be traveling several days to attend the dedication and might hope to receive their temple blessings before returning home. The committee chairman, Brother Sven Eklund, suggested that the Finns could wait a little longer, that Russians could be the first members to perform temple ordinances in the temple. All committee members agreed. Faithful Latter-day Saint Finns delayed their temple blessings to accommodate Russian Saints.

The Area President who was present at that temple committee meeting, Elder Dennis B. Neuenschwander, later wrote: "I have never been prouder of the Finns than I was at this moment. Finland's difficult history with its eastern neighbor . . . and their excitement of finally having [a temple] constructed on their own soil were put aside. Permitting the Russians to enter the temple first [was] a statement of love and sacrifice."[25]

When I reported this kindness to my father, his heart melted and he wept, a very rare occurrence for that stoic Finn. From that time until his death three years later, he never expressed another negative sentiment about Russia. Inspired by the example of his fellow Finns, my father chose to place his discipleship of Jesus Christ above all other considerations. The Finns were no less Finnish; the Russians were no less Russian; neither group abandoned their culture, history, or experiences to banish enmity. They did not need to. Instead, they chose to make their discipleship of Jesus Christ their primary consideration.[26]

If they can do it, so can we. We can bring our heritage, culture, and experiences to the Church of Jesus Christ. Samuel did not shy away from his heritage as a Lamanite,[27] nor did Mormon shy away from his as a Nephite.[28] But each put his discipleship of the Savior first.

If we are not one, we are not His.[29] My invitation is to be valiant in putting our love of God and discipleship of the Savior above all other considerations.[30] Let us uphold the covenant inherent in our discipleship—the covenant to be one.

Let us follow the example of Saints from around the world who are successfully becoming disciples of Christ. We can rely on Jesus Christ, who "is our peace, who . . . hath broken down the middle wall of partition between us; having abolished in his [atoning sacrifice] the enmity."[31] Our witness of Jesus Christ to the world will be strengthened, and we will remain spiritually healthy.[32] I testify that as we "shun contention" and become "like-minded with the Lord in love and united with Him in faith," His peace will be ours.[33] In the name of Jesus Christ, amen.

Notes

1. See "The First Presidency Urges Latter-day Saints to Wear Face Masks When Needed and Get Vaccinated Against COVID-19," Newsroom, Aug. 12, 2021, newsroom.ChurchofJesusChrist .org; "Vaccines Explained," World Health Organization, who.int/emergencies/diseases/novel -coronavirus-2019/covid-19-vaccines/explainers; "Safety of COVID-19 Vaccines," Centers for Disease Control and Prevention, Sept. 27, 2021, cdc.gov/coronavirus/2019-ncov/vaccines /safety/safety-of-vaccines.html; "COVID-19 Vaccine Effectiveness and Safety," *Morbidity and Mortality Weekly Report*, Centers for Disease Control and Prevention, cdc.gov/mmwr/covid19 _vaccine_safety.html.
2. Russell M. Nelson, "Sisters' Participation in the Gathering of Israel," *Ensign* or *Liahona*, Nov. 2018, 69.
3. See Doctrine and Covenants 81:5.
4. Many apostles and prophets have addressed unity and contention over the years. See, for example, Marvin J. Ashton, "No Time for Contention," *Ensign*, May 1978, 7–9; Marion G. Romney, "Unity," *Ensign*, May 1983, 17–18; Russell M. Nelson, "The Canker of Contention," *Ensign*, May 1989, 68–71; Russell M. Nelson, "Children of the Covenant," *Ensign*, May 1995, 32–35; Henry B. Eyring, "That We May Be One," *Ensign*, May 1998, 66–68; D. Todd Christofferson, "Come to Zion," *Ensign* or *Liahona*, Nov. 2008, 37–40; Jeffrey R. Holland, "The Ministry of Reconciliation," *Ensign* or *Liahona*, Nov. 2018, 77–79; Quentin L. Cook, "Hearts Knit in Righteousness and Unity," *Ensign* or *Liahona*, Nov. 2020, 18–22; Gary E. Stevenson, "Hearts Knit Together," *Liahona*, May 2021, 19–23.
5. 3 Nephi 11:28–29.
6. See Moses 7:26, 28, 33. This does not suggest that the Savior's atoning sacrifice is ongoing or that He is continuing to suffer; Jesus Christ has completed the Atonement. However, His infinite and perfect empathy and compassion that He claimed as a result of completing His atoning sacrifice allow Him to feel disappointment and sadness.
7. 2 Nephi 2:8.
8. John 13:34, 35.
9. *Enmity* is the state or feeling of being actively opposed to someone or something; it connotes

hostility, antagonism, animosity, rancor, and deep-seated dislike or ill will. The Greek word translated as "enmity" is also translated as "hatred." It is the opposite of *agape*, which is translated as "love." See James Strong, *The New Strong's Expanded Exhaustive Concordance of the Bible* (2010), Greek dictionary section, number 2189.

10. See John 17:21, 23.
11. 3 Nephi 11:30.
12. 4 Nephi 1:18.
13. 4 Nephi 1:17.
14. 4 Nephi 1:16.
15. President Russell M. Nelson has said, "The Lord loves effort" (in Joy D. Jones, "An Especially Noble Calling," *Ensign* or *Liahona*, May 2020, 16).
16. See 4 Nephi 1:15. There are those who have achieved this kind of unity. In Enoch's day, "the Lord called his people Zion, because they were of one heart and one mind, and dwelt in righteousness; and there was no poor among them" (Moses 7:18).
17. See Mosiah 18:21.
18. See Acts 17:29; Psalm 82:6.
19. See 1 Corinthians 12:12–27.
20. See Moroni 7:47–48.
21. See Doctrine and Covenants 107:30–31.
22. Dallin H. Oaks, "Defending Our Divinely Inspired Constitution," *Liahona*, May 2021, 107.
23. See Romans 14:1–3, 13, 21.
24. The Savior criticized His "disciples, in days of old, [who] sought occasion against one another and forgave not one another in their hearts; and for this evil they were afflicted and sorely chastened. Wherefore," Jesus admonished His latter-day disciples, "I say unto you, that ye ought to forgive one another" (Doctrine and Covenants 64:8–9).
25. Elder Dennis B. Neuenschwander, personal communication.
26. In a typical Finnish fashion, when Brother Eklund discussed this decision, he said it was simply logical. Instead of praising the Finns' magnanimity, he expressed appreciation for the Russians. The Finns were grateful for the significant contribution of the Russians to the work being done in the Helsinki Finland Temple. (Sven Eklund, personal communication.)
27. See Helaman 13:2, 5.
28. See 3 Nephi 5:13, 20.
29. See Doctrine and Covenants 38:27.
30. See Luke 14:25–33.
31. Ephesians 2:14–15.
32. See Ephesians 2:19.
33. See Russell M. Nelson, "The Canker of Contention," *Ensign*, May 1989, 71.

A HOUSE OF SEQUENTIAL ORDER

ELDER VAIANGINA SIKAHEMA
Of the Seventy

In my professional life and in my service in the Church, I have done this thousands of times—just never before the 15 men seated directly behind me. I feel your prayers and theirs.

Brothers and sisters, I am a native of the Kingdom of Tonga in the South Pacific but was raised in North America. The pandemic has kept hundreds, perhaps thousands of young Tongan missionaries serving around the world from returning to their beloved homeland because of its closed borders. Some Tongan elders have been on their missions for three years and sisters over two years! They wait patiently with the faith for which our people are known. Meanwhile, don't be too alarmed if some of them serving in your wards and stakes are looking increasingly more like me—aging and gray. We're grateful for missionaries everywhere for their devoted service, even when longer or shorter than they had anticipated because of the pandemic.

One Sunday when I was a deacon, I was in the foyer with a tray of water passing the sacrament when a woman walked into the building. Dutifully, I approached and handed her the tray. She nodded, smiled, and took a cup of water. She had arrived too late to receive the bread. Shortly after this experience, my home teacher, Ned Brimley, taught me that many aspects and blessings of the gospel of Jesus Christ are given to us in sequential order.

Later that week, Ned and his companion came to our home with a memorable lesson. Ned reminded us that there was order to how God created the earth. The Lord took great care in explaining to Moses the order in which He created the earth. First, He started by dividing the light from the darkness, then water from dry land. He added plant life and animals before introducing to the newly formed planet His greatest creation: humankind, beginning with Adam and Eve.

"So God created man in his own image, in the image of God created he him; male and female created he them. . . .

"And God saw every thing that he had made, and, behold, it was very good" (Genesis 1:27, 31).

The Lord was pleased. And He rested on the seventh day.

The sequential order in which the earth was created gives us a glimpse not only of what is most important to God but also why and for whom He created the earth.

Ned Brimley punctuated his inspired lesson with a simple statement: "Vai, God's house is one of order. He expects you to live your life with order. In proper sequence. He wants you to serve a mission before you get married." To this point, Church leaders currently teach that "the Lord expects each able young man to prepare to serve. . . . Young women . . . who desire to serve should also prepare" (*General Handbook: Serving in The Church of Jesus Christ of Latter-day Saints*, 24.0, ChurchofJesusChrist.org). Brother Brimley continued: "God wants you to get married before you have children. And He wants you to continually develop your talents as you earn an education." If you choose to live your life out of sequence, you will find life more difficult and chaotic.

Brother Brimley also taught us that through His atoning sacrifice, the Savior helps us to restore order to our lives made chaotic or out of sequence by our own or others' poor choices.

From that time on, I've had a fascination with "sequential order." I developed a habit of looking for sequential patterns in life and in the gospel.

Elder David A. Bednar taught this principle: "As we study, learn, and live the gospel of Jesus Christ, sequence often is instructive. Consider, for example, the lessons we learn about spiritual priorities from the order of the major events that occurred as the fulness of the Savior's gospel was restored in these latter days."

Elder Bednar listed the First Vision and Moroni's initial appearance to Joseph Smith as teaching the boy prophet first, the nature and character of God, followed by the role the Book of Mormon and Elijah would play in gathering Israel on both sides of the veil in this last dispensation.

Elder Bednar concludes: "This inspiring sequence is instructive about the spiritual matters of highest priority to Deity" ("The Hearts of the Children Shall Turn," *Ensign* or *Liahona*, Nov. 2011, 24).

One observation I've made is that "sequential order" is a simple, natural, and effective way for the Lord to teach us, as His children, important principles.

We've come to earth to learn and gain experience we would not otherwise have. Our growth is unique to each of us individually and a vital component of Heavenly Father's plan. Our physical and spiritual growth begins in stages and develops slowly as we gain experience sequentially.

Alma gives a powerful sermon on faith—drawing on the analogy of a seed, which, if tended and nourished properly, sprouts from a small sapling into a full-grown, mature tree that produces delicious fruit (see Alma 32:28–43). The lesson is that your faith will increase as you give place for and nourish the seed—or the word of God—in your hearts. Your faith will increase as the word of God begins "to swell within your breasts" (verse 28). That it "swelleth, and sprouteth, and beginneth to grow" (verse 30) is both visual and instructive. It is also sequential.

The Lord teaches us individually according to our capacity to learn and how we learn. Our growth is dependent on our willingness, natural curiosity, level of faith, and understanding.

Nephi was taught what Joseph Smith would learn in Kirtland, Ohio, over 2,300 years later: "For behold, thus saith the Lord God: I will give unto the children of men line upon line, precept upon precept, here a little and there a little; and blessed are those who hearken unto my precepts, and lend an ear unto my counsel, for they shall learn wisdom" (2 Nephi 28:30).

That we learn "line upon line, precept upon precept, here a little and there a little" is again sequential.

Consider the following statements we've heard most of our lives: "First things first" or "Feed them milk before meat." How about

"We have to walk before we run"? Each of these axioms describes something that is sequential.

Miracles operate according to sequential order. Miracles occur when we first exercise faith. Faith precedes the miracle.

Young men are also ordained to offices of the Aaronic Priesthood in sequence, according to the age of the one being ordained: deacon, teacher, and then priest.

The ordinances of salvation and exaltation are sequential in nature. We are baptized prior to receiving the gift of the Holy Ghost. Temple ordinances are similarly sequential. Of course, as my friend Ned Brimley so wisely taught me, the sacrament is sequential—it begins with the bread, followed by the water.

"And as they were eating, Jesus took bread, and blessed it, and brake it, and gave it to the disciples, and said, Take, eat; this is my body.

"And he took the cup, and gave thanks, and gave it to them, saying, Drink ye all of it;

"For this is my blood of the new testament, which is shed for many for the remission of sins" (Matthew 26:26–28).

In Jerusalem and in the Americas, the Savior instituted the sacrament in the exact same order.

"Behold, mine house is a house of order, saith the Lord God, and not a house of confusion" (Doctrine and Covenants 132:8).

Repentance is sequential. It begins with faith in Jesus Christ, even if just a particle. Faith requires humility, which is an essential element of having a "broken heart and a contrite spirit" (2 Nephi 2:7).

Indeed, the first four principles of the gospel are sequential. "We believe that the first principles and ordinances of the Gospel are: first, Faith in the Lord Jesus Christ; second, Repentance; third, Baptism by immersion for the remission of sins; fourth, Laying on of hands for the gift of the Holy Ghost" (Articles of Faith 1:4).

King Benjamin taught his people this important truth: "And see that all these things are done in wisdom and order; for it is not requisite that a man should run faster than he has strength. And again, it is expedient that he should be diligent, that thereby he might win the prize; therefore, all things must be done in order" (Mosiah 4:27).

May we live our lives with order and seek to follow the sequence the Lord has outlined for us. We will be blessed as we look for and follow the patterns and the sequence in which the Lord teaches what's most important to Him. In the sacred name of Jesus Christ, amen.

PERSONAL PEACE IN CHALLENGING TIMES

ELDER QUENTIN L. COOK

Of the Quorum of the Twelve Apostles

I was recently assigned to dedicate a portion of historic Nauvoo. As part of the assignment, I was able to visit Liberty Jail in Missouri. As I viewed the jail, I contemplated the events that make it such a significant part of Church history. The lives of the Saints were threatened as the result of an extermination order issued by the governor of Missouri. In addition, the Prophet Joseph and a few choice associates had been unjustly imprisoned in Liberty Jail. One of the reasons for the violent opposition to our members was most of them were opposed to slavery.[1] This intense persecution of Joseph Smith and his followers constitutes an extreme example of the unrighteous exercise of agency that can impact righteous people. Joseph's time in Liberty Jail demonstrates that adversity is not evidence of the Lord's disfavor nor a withdrawal of His blessings.

I was deeply moved as I read what the Prophet Joseph Smith declared as he was confined in Liberty Jail: "O God, where art thou? And where is the pavilion that covereth thy hiding place?"[2] Joseph inquired how long the Lord's people would "suffer these wrongs and unlawful oppressions."[3]

As I stood in Liberty Jail, I was deeply touched as I read the Lord's answer: "My son, peace be unto thy soul; thine adversity and thine afflictions shall be but a small moment; and then, if thou endure it well, God shall exalt thee on high."[4] It is clear that opposition can refine us for an eternal, celestial destiny.[5]

The Savior's precious words "My son, peace be unto thy soul"[6] resonate with me personally and have great significance for our day. They remind me of His teachings to His disciples during His mortal ministry.

Prior to Christ's suffering in the Garden of Gethsemane and on the cross, He commanded His Apostles to "love one another; as I have loved you"[7] and subsequently comforted them with these

142

words: "Peace I leave with you, my peace I give unto you: not as the world giveth, give I unto you. Let not your heart be troubled, neither let it be afraid."[8]

One of the most cherished titles of our Lord and Savior, Jesus Christ, is "Prince of Peace."[9] Ultimately His kingdom will be established including peace and love.[10] We look forward to the millennial reign of the Messiah.

Notwithstanding this vision of the millennial reign, we know that world peace and harmony are not prevalent in our day.[11] In my lifetime, I have never seen a greater lack of civility. We are bombarded with angry, contentious language and provocative, devastating actions that destroy peace and tranquility.

Peace in the world is not promised or assured until the Second Coming of Jesus Christ. The Savior instructed His Apostles that His earthly mission would not achieve universal peace. He taught, "Think not that I am come to send peace on earth."[12] Universal peace was not part of the Savior's initial mortal ministry. Universal peace does not exist today.

However, *personal* peace can be achieved despite the anger, contention, and division that blight and corrupt our world today. It has never been more important to seek personal peace. A beautiful and beloved new hymn, written for today's youth by Brother Nik Day, titled "Peace in Christ" declares, "When there's no peace on earth, there is peace in Christ."[13] We were blessed to have this hymn just before the worldwide COVID-19 pandemic.

This hymn reflects in a beautiful fashion the aspiration for peace and appropriately emphasizes that peace is anchored in the life and mission of Jesus Christ. President Joseph F. Smith declared, "There never can come to the world that spirit of peace and love . . . until mankind will receive God's truth and God's message . . . and acknowledge his power and authority which is divine."[14]

While we will never retreat from efforts to achieve universal peace, we have been assured that we can have personal peace, as Christ teaches. This principle is set forth in the Doctrine and Covenants: "But learn that he who doeth the works of righteousness shall receive his reward, even peace in this world, and eternal life in the world to come."[15]

What are some of the "works of righteousness" that will help us deal with disputations and lessen contention and find peace in this world? All of Christ's teachings point in this direction. I will mention a few which I believe are particularly important.

First: Love God, Live His Commandments, and Forgive Everyone

President George Albert Smith became President of the Church in 1945. He had been known during his years as an Apostle as a peace-loving leader. In the preceding 15 years before he became President, the challenges and trials of a massive worldwide depression, followed by the death and destruction of World War II, had been anything but peaceful.

At the conclusion of World War II, during his first general conference as President in October 1945, President Smith reminded the Saints of the Savior's invitation to love their neighbors and forgive their enemies and then taught, "That is the spirit all Latter-day Saints should seek to possess if they hope some day to stand in his presence and receive at his hands a glorious welcome home."[16]

Second: Seek the Fruits of the Spirit

The Apostle Paul, in his Epistle to the Galatians, sets forth the dichotomy between works of righteousness that qualify us to inherit the kingdom of God and works that can, without repentance, disqualify us. Among those that qualify us are the fruits of the Spirit: "love, joy, peace, longsuffering, gentleness, goodness, faith, meekness, [and] temperance."[17] Paul also includes bearing one another's burdens and being not weary in well-doing.[18] Among those works that are not righteous he includes hatred, wrath, and *strife*.[19]

One of the great lessons in the Old Testament period relates to Father Abraham. Abraham and Lot, his nephew, were wealthy but found they could not dwell together. To eliminate strife, Abraham allowed Lot to choose the land he wanted. Lot chose the plain of

Jordan, which was both well watered and beautiful. Abraham took the less fertile plain of Mamre. The scriptures read that Abraham then pitched his tent and built "an altar unto the Lord."[20] Lot, on the other hand, "pitched his tent toward Sodom."[21] To have peaceful relationships, the lesson is clear: we should be willing to compromise and eliminate strife with respect to matters that do not involve righteousness. As King Benjamin taught, "Ye will not have a mind to injure one another, but to live peaceably."[22] But on conduct relating to righteousness and doctrinal imperatives, we need to remain firm and steadfast.

If we want to have the peace which is the reward of the works of righteousness, we will *not* pitch our tents toward the world. We will pitch our tents toward the temple.

Third: Exercise Agency to Choose Righteousness

Peace and agency are intertwined as essential elements of the plan of salvation. As described in the Gospel Topics article "Agency and Accountability," "Agency is the ability and privilege God gives us to choose and to act for ourselves."[23] Thus, agency is at the heart of the personal growth and experience that bless us as we follow the Savior.[24]

Agency was a principal issue in the premortal Council in Heaven and the conflict between those who chose to follow Christ and the followers of Satan.[25] Letting go of pride and control and choosing the Savior would allow us to have His light and His peace. But personal peace would be challenged when people exercised their agency in harmful and hurtful ways.

I am confident that the peaceful assurance we felt in our hearts was strengthened by the knowledge we had of what the Savior of the world would accomplish in our behalf. This is beautifully set forth in *Preach My Gospel*: "As we rely on the Atonement of Jesus Christ, He can help us endure our trials, sicknesses, and pain. We can be filled with joy, *peace*, and consolation. All that is unfair about life can be made right through the Atonement of Jesus Christ."[26]

Fourth: Build Zion in Our Hearts and Homes

We are children of God and part of His family. We are also part of the family into which we are born. The institution of the family is the foundation for both happiness and peace. President Russell M. Nelson has taught us—and during this pandemic we have learned—that the home-centered, Church-supported religious observance can "unleash the power of families . . . to transform [our] home[s] into a sanctuary of faith."[27] If we have this religious observance in our homes, we will also have the Savior's peace.[28] We are aware that many of you do not have the blessings of righteous homes and contend regularly with those who choose unrighteousness. The Savior can provide protection and peace to guide you ultimately to safety and shelter from life's storms.

I assure you that the joy, love, and fulfillment experienced in loving, righteous families produce both peace and happiness. Love and kindness are at the center of having Zion in our hearts and homes.[29]

Fifth: Follow the Current Admonitions of Our Prophet

Our peace is greatly enhanced when we follow the Lord's prophet, President Russell M. Nelson. We will shortly have an opportunity to hear from him. He was prepared from the foundations of the world for this calling. His personal preparation has been most remarkable.[30]

He has taught us that we can "feel enduring peace and joy, even during turbulent times," as we strive to become more like our Savior, Jesus Christ.[31] He has counseled us to "repent daily" to receive the Lord's "cleansing, healing, and strengthening power."[32] I am a personal witness that revelation has been received and continues to be received from heaven by our beloved prophet.

While we honor and sustain him as our prophet, we worship our Heavenly Father and our Savior, Jesus Christ. We are ministered to by the Holy Ghost.

I testify and provide my personal apostolic witness that Jesus

Christ, the Savior and Redeemer of the world, leads and guides His restored Church. His life and atoning mission are the true source of peace. He is the Prince of Peace. I bear my sure and solemn witness that He lives. In the name of Jesus Christ, amen.

Notes

1. "People in Independence did not like that the Saints preached to Indians and disapproved of slavery" (*Saints: The Story of the Church of Jesus Christ in the Latter Days*, vol. 1, *The Standard of Truth, 1815–1846* [2018], 172).
2. Doctrine and Covenants 121:1.
3. Doctrine and Covenants 121:3.
4. Doctrine and Covenants 121:7–8.
5. See 2 Nephi 2:11–15.
6. Doctrine and Covenants 121:7.
7. John 13:34.
8. John 14:27.
9. Isaiah 9:6; 2 Nephi 19:6. The Savior, in His Beatitudes, also taught, "Blessed are the peacemakers: for they shall be called the children of God" (Matthew 5:9).
10. "With judgment and with justice . . . for ever" (see Isaiah 9:6–7; 2 Nephi 19:6–7; see also Galatians 5:22).
11. See Doctrine and Covenants 1:35. President Wilford Woodruff declared this in 1894 and again in 1896 (see *The Discourses of Wilford Woodruff*, sel. G. Homer Durham [1946], 251–52; see also Marion G. Romney, in Conference Report, Apr. 1967, 79–82; Ezra Taft Benson, "The Power of the Word," *Ensign*, May 1986, 79–80; Dallin H. Oaks, "Preparation for the Second Coming," *Ensign* or *Liahona*, May 2004, 9).
12. Matthew 10:34.
13. Nik Day, "Peace in Christ," 2018 Mutual theme song, *Liahona*, Jan. 2018, 54–55; *New Era*, Jan. 2018, 24–25. The hymn "Peace in Christ" teaches:

    > *When we live the way He lived,*
    > *There is peace in Christ.*
    > *He gives us hope*
    > *When hope is gone.*
    > *He gives us strength*
    > *When we can't go on.*
    > *He gives us shelter*
    > *In the storms of life.*
    > *When there's no peace on earth,*
    > *There is peace in Christ.*

14. *Teachings of Presidents of the Church: Joseph F. Smith* (1998), 400.
15. Doctrine and Covenants 59:23.
16. See George Albert Smith, in Conference Report, Oct. 1945, 169–70.
17. Galatians 5:22–23.
18. See Galatians 6:2, 9.
19. See Galatians 5:20.
20. Genesis 13:18.
21. Genesis 13:12.
22. Mosiah 4:13.
23. Gospel Topics, "Agency and Accountability," topics.ChurchofJesusChrist.org.
24. We are "free to choose liberty and eternal life, through the great Mediator of all men" (2 Nephi 2:27). Agency also allows the devastating evil choices of others to cause pain and suffering and sometimes even death. The scriptures make it clear that the Lord God gave agency so that man could choose good or evil (see 2 Nephi 2:16).
25. See Gospel Topics, "Agency and Accountability," topics.ChurchofJesusChrist.org.

26. *Preach My Gospel: A Guide to Missionary Service* (2019), 52, ChurchofJesusChrist.org; emphasis added.

27. Russell M. Nelson, "Becoming Exemplary Latter-day Saints," *Ensign* or *Liahona*, Nov. 2018, 113.

28. See Doctrine and Covenants 19:23.

29. I was fortunate to grow up in a home where peace prevailed. This was primarily due to the influence of our mother, who was a faithful member of the Church. My father was outstanding in every way but was less active. Mother honored our father and avoided contention. She taught us as children to pray and attend church. She also taught us to love and serve each other (see Mosiah 4:14–15). Growing up in such a home provided peace and has been a great blessing in my life.

30. Russell M. Nelson graduated from the University of Utah Medical School first in his class at age 22. He had long desired to be a surgeon and received the best training available at major medical institutions. He faithfully fulfilled military commitments in Korea and Japan. For many years he was a pioneer in open-heart surgery and was recognized worldwide. As remarkable as this preparation was to bless people all over the world with his medical skills, President Nelson's spiritual preparation was even more important. He is the father of a large family of children, grandchildren, and great-grandchildren. He has faithfully served his family and Church throughout his life.

31. See Russell M. Nelson, "Opening Message," *Ensign* or *Liahona*, May 2020, 6; see also Russell M. Nelson, "Joy and Spiritual Survival," *Ensign* or *Liahona*, Nov. 2016, 81–84.

32. Russell M. Nelson, "Opening Message," 6.

THE TEMPLE AND YOUR SPIRITUAL FOUNDATION

PRESIDENT RUSSELL M. NELSON

President of The Church of Jesus Christ of Latter-day Saints

My dear brothers and sisters, I am grateful to be with you this morning to share the feelings of my heart.

As you know, we are performing major renovations on the historic Salt Lake Temple. This complex project includes major reinforcement of its original foundation, which has served well for more than a century. But this temple must stand much longer. In late May, I inspected the progress on this massive project. I thought you would appreciate seeing what my wife Wendy and I saw. I think you'll see why the hymn "How Firm a Foundation"[1] has come to have new meaning for us.

Video from the site of the Salt Lake Temple renovation: "We are looking at the original foundation of the Salt Lake Temple. I am standing in an area beneath what was the Garden Room. As I examine the craftsmanship of this entire building, I marvel at what the pioneers accomplished. I am totally in awe when I consider that they built this magnificent temple with only tools and techniques available to them more than a century ago.

"These many decades later, however, if we examine the foundation closely, we can see the effects of erosion, gaps in the original stonework, and varying stages of stability in the masonry.

"Now as I witness what modern engineers, architects, and construction experts can do to reinforce that original foundation, I am absolutely amazed. Their work is astonishing!

"The foundation of any building, particularly one as large as this one, must be strong and resilient enough to withstand earthquakes, corrosion, high winds, and the inevitable settling that affects all buildings. The complex task of strengthening now underway will reinforce this sacred temple with the foundation that can and will stand the test of time."

We are sparing no effort to give this venerable temple, which had become increasingly *vulnerable*, a foundation that will withstand the forces of nature into the Millennium. In like manner, it is now time that we each implement extraordinary measures—perhaps measures we have never taken before—to strengthen our *personal spiritual* foundations. Unprecedented times call for unprecedented measures.

My dear brothers and sisters, these *are* the latter days. If you and I are to withstand the forthcoming perils and pressures, it is imperative that we each have a *firm* spiritual foundation built upon the rock of our Redeemer, Jesus Christ.[2]

So I ask each of you, how firm is *your* foundation? And what reinforcements to your testimony and understanding of the gospel are needed?

The temple lies at the center of strengthening our faith and spiritual fortitude because the Savior and His doctrine are the very heart of the temple. Everything taught in the temple, through instruction and through the Spirit, increases our understanding of Jesus Christ. His essential ordinances bind us to Him through sacred priesthood covenants. Then, as we keep our covenants, He endows us with *His* healing, strengthening power.[3] And oh, how we will need His power in the days ahead.

We have been promised that "if [we] are prepared [we] shall not fear."[4] This assurance has profound implications today. The Lord has declared that despite today's unprecedented challenges, those who build their foundations upon Jesus Christ, and have learned how to draw upon His power, need not succumb to the unique anxieties of this era.

Temple ordinances and covenants are ancient. The Lord instructed Adam and Eve to pray, make covenants, and offer sacrifices.[5] Indeed, "whenever the Lord has had a people on the earth who will obey His word, they have been commanded to build temples."[6] The standard works are replete with references to temple teachings, clothing, language, and more.[7] *Everything* we believe and *every* promise God has made to His covenant people come together in the temple. In *every* age, the temple has underscored the precious truth that those who make covenants with God and keep them are children of the covenant.

Thus, in the house of the Lord, we can make the same covenants with God that Abraham, Isaac, and Jacob made. And we can receive the same blessings!

Temples have been part of *this* dispensation from its earliest days.[8] Elijah committed the keys of sealing authority to Joseph Smith in the Kirtland Temple. The fulness of the priesthood was restored in the Nauvoo Temple.[9]

Until his martyrdom, Joseph Smith continued to receive revelations that furthered the restoration of the endowment and sealing ordinances.[10] He recognized, however, that further refinement was needed. After administering the endowment to Brigham Young in May 1842, Joseph told Brigham, "This is not arranged right, but we have done the best we could under the circumstances in which we are placed, and I wish you to take this matter in hand and organize and systematize all these ceremonies."[11]

Following the Prophet's death, President Young oversaw the completion of the Nauvoo Temple[12] and later built temples in the Utah Territory. At the dedication of the lower stories of the St. George Temple, Brigham Young vigorously declared the urgency of vicarious temple work when he said, "When I think upon this subject, I want the tongues of seven thunders to wake up the people."[13]

From that time forward, temple ordinances were gradually refined. President Harold B. Lee explained why procedures, policies, and even the administration of temple ordinances continue to change within the Savior's restored Church. President Lee said: "The principles of the gospel of Jesus Christ are divine. Nobody changes the principles and [doctrine] of the Church except the Lord by revelation. But methods change as the inspired direction comes to those who preside at a given time."[14]

Consider how administering the sacrament has changed over the years. In earlier days, the water of the sacrament was offered to the congregation in one large vessel. Everyone drank from it. Now we use individual disposable cups. The procedure changed, but the covenants remain the same.

Ponder these three truths:

1. The Restoration is a process, not an event, and will continue until the Lord comes again.
2. The ultimate objective of the gathering of Israel[15] is to bring the blessings of the temple to God's faithful children.
3. As we seek how to accomplish *that* objective more effectively, the Lord reveals more insights. The ongoing Restoration needs ongoing revelation.

The First Presidency and Quorum of the Twelve Apostles have often asked the Lord if there are better ways to take the blessings of the temple to His faithful children. We seek guidance regularly on how to ensure worldwide accuracy and consistency of temple instruction, covenants, and ordinances despite differences in language and culture.

Under the Lord's direction and in answer to our prayers, recent procedural adjustments have been made. *He* is the One who wants you to understand with great clarity exactly what you are making covenants to do. *He* is the One who wants you to experience fully *His* sacred ordinances. *He* wants you to comprehend your privileges, promises, and responsibilities. *He* wants you to have spiritual insights and awakenings you've never had before. This He desires for *all* temple patrons, no matter where they live.

Current adjustments in temple procedures, and others that will follow, are continuing evidence that the Lord is actively directing His Church. He is providing opportunities for each of us to bolster our spiritual foundations more effectively by centering our lives on Him and on the ordinances and covenants of His temple. When you bring your temple recommend, a contrite heart, and a seeking mind to the Lord's house of learning, *He* will teach you.

Should distance, health challenges, or other constraints prohibit your temple attendance for a season, I invite you to set a regular time to rehearse in your mind the covenants you have made.

If you don't yet love to attend the temple, go more often—not less. Let the Lord, through His Spirit, teach and inspire you there. I promise you that over time, the temple will become a place of safety, solace, and revelation.

If it were possible for me to speak one-on-one with every young adult, I would plead with you to seek a companion with whom you can be sealed in the temple. You may wonder what difference this will make in your life. I promise it will make *all* the difference! As you marry in the temple and return repeatedly, you will be strengthened and guided in your decisions.

If I could speak with each husband and wife who have *still* not been sealed in the temple, I would plead with you to take the necessary steps to receive that crowning, life-changing ordinance.[16] Will it make a difference? Only if you want to progress forever and be together forever. *Wishing* to be together forever will not make it so. No other ceremony or contract will make it so.[17]

If I could speak to each man or woman who longs for marriage but has not yet found his or her eternal companion, I would urge you not to wait until marriage to be endowed in the house of the Lord. Begin now to learn and experience what it means to be armed with priesthood power.

And to each of you who has made temple covenants, I plead with you to seek—prayerfully and consistently—to understand temple covenants and ordinances.[18] Spiritual doors will open. You will learn how to part the veil between heaven and earth, how to ask for God's angels to attend you, and how better to receive direction from heaven. Your diligent efforts to do so will reinforce and strengthen your spiritual foundation.

My dear brothers and sisters, when renovations on the Salt Lake Temple are completed, there will be *no safer* place during an earthquake in the Salt Lake Valley than inside that temple.

Likewise, whenever any kind of upheaval occurs in your life, the safest place to be *spiritually* is living *inside* your temple covenants!

Please believe me when I say that when your spiritual foundation is built solidly upon Jesus Christ, you have *no need to fear*. As you are true to your covenants made in the temple, you will be strengthened by His power. Then, when spiritual earthquakes occur, you will be able to stand *strong* because your spiritual foundation is solid and immovable.

I love you, dear brothers and sisters. These truths I know: God, our Heavenly Father, wants *you* to choose to come home to Him. His plan of eternal progression is not complicated, and it honors your agency. You are free to choose who you will be—and with whom you will be—in the world to come!

God lives! Jesus is the Christ! This is His Church, restored to help you fulfill your divine destiny. I so testify in the sacred name of Jesus Christ, amen.

Notes

1. See "How Firm a Foundation," *Hymns*, no. 85.
2. So that "when the devil [sends] forth his mighty [wind], . . . it shall have no power over [us] . . . because of the rock upon which [we] are built, which is a *sure foundation*, a foundation whereon if men build they cannot fall" (Helaman 5:12; emphasis added).
3. See Doctrine and Covenants 109:15, 22.
4. Doctrine and Covenants 38:30; see also Doctrine and Covenants 10:55.
5. See Moses 5:5–6.
6. Bible Dictionary, "Temple."
7. For example, see Exodus 28; 29; Leviticus 8. The tabernacle of Moses was known as a "tent of the testimony" (Numbers 9:15) and a "tabernacle of testimony" (Exodus 38:21). Solomon's temple was destroyed in 587 BC, a few years after Lehi's family left Jerusalem. The restoration of this temple by Zerubbabel took place some 70 years later. It was then damaged by fire in 37 BC. Herod expanded the temple in about 16 BC. Then this temple, known by Jesus, was destroyed in AD 70. Nephi had temple-like experiences by going "into the mount oft" to pray (1 Nephi 18:3) and later, in the Americas, built a temple "after the manner of the temple of Solomon," though it was less ornate (see 2 Nephi 5:16).
8. See Doctrine and Covenants 88:119; 124:31.
9. See Doctrine and Covenants 110:13–16; 124:28. The cornerstone for the Nauvoo Temple was laid on April 6, 1841, just a few months after Joseph Smith received the revelation to build it. The Nauvoo Temple had augmented functions. For example, the Lord explained that a baptismal font was needed for the Saints to be baptized for those who were dead (see Doctrine and Covenants 124:29–30).
10. See Doctrine and Covenants 131; 132. Doctrine and Covenants 128 contains an epistle Joseph Smith wrote to the Saints concerning baptism for the dead. There he declared that the salvation of the dead "is necessary and essential to our salvation, . . . [for] they without us cannot be made perfect—neither can we without our dead be made perfect" (verse 15).
11. Joseph Smith, in *Saints: The Story of the Church of Jesus Christ in the Latter Days*, vol. 1, *The Standard of Truth, 1815–1846* (2018), 454.
12. "Church Historian George A. Smith concluded that 5,634 brothers and sisters received their endowment in the partially completed Nauvoo Temple in December 1845 and January 1846. Sealings of couples continued on through Feb. 7, [1846,] by which time more than 2,000 couples had been united by the priesthood for time and eternity" (Bruce A. Van Orden,

"Temple Finished before Exodus," *Deseret News*, Dec. 9, 1995, deseret.com; see also Richard O. Cowan, "Endowments Bless the Living and Dead," *Church News*, Aug. 27, 1988, thechurchnews.com).

13. "What do you suppose the fathers would say if they could speak from the dead? Would they not say, 'We have lain here thousands of years, here in this prison house, waiting for this dispensation to come'? . . . Why, if they had the power the very thunders of heaven would be in our ears, if we could but realize the importance of the work we are engaged in. All the angels in heaven are looking at this little handful of people, and stimulating them to the salvation of the human family. . . . When I think upon this subject, I want the tongues of seven thunders to wake up the people" (*Discourses of Brigham Young*, sel. John A. Widtsoe [1954], 403–4).

14. Harold B. Lee, "God's Kingdom—a Kingdom of Order," *Ensign*, Jan. 1971, 10. See also a statement made by President Wilford Woodruff in 1896; he declared: "I want to say, as the president of the Church of Jesus Christ of Latter-day Saints, that we should now go on and progress. We have not [gotten] through with revelation. . . . President [Brigham] Young, who followed President Joseph Smith, led us here. He organized these temples and carried out the purposes of his calling and office. . . . He did not receive all the revelations that belong to this work; neither did President Taylor, nor has Wilford Woodruff. There will be no end to this work until it is perfected" (*The Discourses of Wilford Woodruff*, sel. G. Homer Durham [1946], 153–54).

15. See 3 Nephi 29:8–9.

16. See Doctrine and Covenants 131:2, 4.

17. See Doctrine and Covenants 132:7.

18. Elder John A. Widtsoe wrote: "To the man or woman who goes through the temple, with open eyes, heeding the symbols and the covenants, and making a steady, continuous effort to understand the full meaning, God speaks his word, and revelations come. The endowment is so richly symbolic that only a fool would attempt to describe it; it is so packed full of revelations to those who exercise their strength to seek and see, that no human words can explain or make clear the possibilities that reside in temple service. The endowment which was given by revelation can best be understood by revelation" (in Archibald F. Bennett, *Saviors on Mount Zion* [Sunday School manual, 1950], 168).

SUNDAY AFTERNOON SESSION

OCTOBER 3, 2021

TRUST AGAIN

ELDER GERRIT W. GONG
Of the Quorum of the Twelve Apostles

Once, when I was very young, I briefly thought about running away from home. In a little-boy way, I felt no one loved me.

My observant mother listened and assured me. I was safely home.

Have you ever felt like you are running from home? Often, running from home means trust has been frayed or broken—trust with ourselves, with each other, with God. When trust is challenged, we wonder how to trust again.

My message today is, whether we are coming home or going home, God is coming to meet us.[1] In Him we can find faith and courage, wisdom and discernment to trust again. Likewise, He asks us to keep the light on for each other, to be more forgiving and less judgmental of ourselves and each other, so His Church can be a place where we feel at home, whether we are coming for the first time or returning.

Trust is an act of faith. God keeps faith with us. Yet, human trust can be undermined or broken when:

- A friend, business associate, or someone we trust isn't truthful, hurts us, or takes advantage of us.[2]
- A marriage partner is unfaithful.
- Perhaps unexpectedly, someone we love confronts death, injury, or illness.
- We face an unanticipated gospel question, perhaps something regarding Church history or Church policy, and someone says our church somehow hid or did not tell the truth.

Other situations may be less specific but of equal concern.

Perhaps we don't see ourselves in the Church, don't feel we fit, feel judged by others.

Or, though we have done everything expected, things have yet

157

to work out. Despite our personal experiences with the Holy Ghost, we may not yet feel we know God lives or the gospel is true.

Many today feel a great need to restore trust in human relationships and modern society.[3]

As we reflect on trust, we know God is a God of truth and "canst not lie."[4] We know truth is a knowledge of things as they are, were, and are to come.[5] We know continuing revelation and inspiration fit unchanging truth to changing circumstances.

We know broken covenants break hearts. "I did stupid things," he says. "Can you ever forgive me?" The husband and wife may hold hands, hoping to trust again. In a different setting, a prison inmate reflects, "If I had kept the Word of Wisdom, I would not be here today."

We know that joy on the Lord's covenant path and callings to serve in His Church are an invitation to feel God's trust and love for us and each other. Church members, including single adults, regularly serve across the Church and in our communities.

By inspiration, a bishopric calls a young couple to serve in the ward nursery. At first, the husband sits in the corner, detached and distant. Gradually, he begins smiling with the children. Later, the couple expresses gratitude. Earlier, they say, the wife wanted children; the husband did not. Now, serving has changed and united them. It has also brought the joy of children into their marriage and home.

In another city, a young mother with little children and her husband are surprised and overwhelmed but accept when she is called to serve as ward Relief Society president. Shortly thereafter, ice storms cut electric power, leaving store shelves empty and homes as cold as iceboxes. Because they have power and heat, this young family generously opens their home to several families and individuals to weather the storm.

Trust becomes real when we do hard things with faith. Service and sacrifice increase capacity and refine hearts. Trust in God and each other brings heaven's blessings.

After surviving cancer, a faithful brother is hit by a car. Instead of feeling sorry for himself, he prayerfully asks, "What can I learn from this experience?" In his intensive care unit, he feels prompted to notice a nurse worried for her husband and children. A patient in pain finds answers as he trusts God and reaches out to others.

As a brother with pornography concerns waits outside his stake president's office, the stake president prays to know how to help. A clear impression comes: "Open the door and let the brother in." With faith and trust God will help, the priesthood leader opens the door and embraces the brother. Each feels transforming love and trust for God and each other. Fortified, the brother can begin to repent and change.

While our individual circumstances are personal, gospel principles and the Holy Ghost can help us know if, how, and when to trust in others again. When trust is broken or betrayed, disappointment and disillusionment are real; so is the need for discernment to know when faith and courage are merited to trust again in human relations.

Yet, with respect to God and personal revelation, President Russell M. Nelson assures, "You do not have to wonder whom you can safely trust."[6] We can always trust God. The Lord knows us better and loves us more than we know or love ourselves. His infinite love and perfect knowledge of past, present, and future make His covenants and promises constant and sure.

Trust what the scriptures call "in process of time."[7] With God's blessing, process of time, and continuing faith and obedience, we can find resolution and peace.

The Lord comforts:

"Weeping may endure for a night, but joy cometh in the morning."[8]

"Cast your burdens [upon] the Lord and trust his constant care."[9]

"Earth has no sorrow that heav'n cannot heal."[10]

Trust God[11] and His miracles. We and our relationships can change. Through the Atonement of Christ the Lord, we can put off our selfish natural self and become a child of God, meek, humble,[12] full of faith and appropriate trust. When we repent, when we confess and forsake our sins, the Lord says He remembers them no more.[13] It is not that He forgets; rather, in a remarkable way, it seems He chooses not to remember them, nor need we.

Trust God's inspiration to discern wisely. We can forgive others in the right time and way, as the Lord says we must,[14] while being "wise as serpents, and harmless as doves."[15]

Sometimes when our hearts are most broken and contrite, we are most open to the comfort and guidance of the Holy Ghost.[16] Condemnation and forgiveness both begin by recognizing a wrong. Often condemnation focuses on the past. Forgiveness looks liberatingly to the future. "For God sent not his Son into the world to condemn the world; but that the world through him might be saved."[17]

The Apostle Paul asks, "Who shall separate us from the love of Christ?" He answers, "Neither death, nor life, . . . nor height, nor depth . . . shall be able to separate us from the love of God, which is in Christ Jesus our Lord."[18] Yet, there is someone who can separate us from God and Jesus Christ—and that someone is us, ourselves. As Isaiah says, "Your sins have hid his face from you."[19]

By divine love and divine law, we are responsible for our choices and their consequences. But our Savior's atoning love is "infinite and eternal."[20] When we are ready to come home, even when we are "yet a great way off,"[21] God is ready with great compassion to welcome us, joyfully offering the best He has.[22]

President J. Reuben Clark said, "I believe that our Heavenly Father wants to save every one of his children, . . . that in his justice and mercy he will give us the maximum reward for our acts, give us all that he can give, and in the reverse, I believe that he will impose upon us the minimum penalty which it is possible for him to impose."[23]

On the cross, even our Savior's merciful plea to His Father was not an unconditional "Father, forgive them" but rather "Father, forgive them; for they know not what they do."[24] Our agency and freedom have meaning because we are accountable before God and ourselves for who we are, for what we know and do. Thankfully, we can trust God's perfect justice and perfect mercy to judge perfectly our intents and actions.

We conclude as we began—with God's compassion as we each come home to Him and each other.

Do you remember Jesus Christ's parable about a certain man who had two sons?[25] One son left home and wasted his inheritance. When he came to himself, this son sought to come home. The other son, feeling he had kept the commandments "lo, these many years,"[26] did not want to welcome his brother home.

Brothers and sisters, would you please consider Jesus is asking us to open our hearts, our understanding, compassion, and humility, and to see ourselves in both roles?

Like the first son or daughter, we may wander and later seek to return home. God waits to welcome us.

And like the other son or daughter, we are gently entreated by God to rejoice together as we each come home to Him. He invites us to make our congregations, quorums, classes, and activities open, authentic, safe—home for each other. With kindness, understanding, and mutual respect, we each humbly seek the Lord and pray and welcome His restored gospel blessings for all.

Our life journeys are individual, but we can come again to God our Father and His Beloved Son through trust in God, each other, and ourselves.[27] Jesus beckons, "Be not afraid, only believe."[28] As did the Prophet Joseph, undaunted may we trust in our Heavenly Father's care.[29] Dear brother, dear sister, dear friend, please look again for faith and trust—a miracle He promises you today. In the sacred and holy name of Jesus Christ, amen.

Notes

1. See Luke 15:20.
2. For example, I know and admire individuals who work honorably for years to repay heavy business debts left to them by others.
3. Trust is an essential element of human capital in society and contributes to economic, social, and political prosperity and well-being (see, for example, Francis Fukuyama, *Trust: The Social Virtues and the Creation of Prosperity* [1995], 3–59).
4. Ether 3:12; see also Enos 1:6.
5. See Doctrine and Covenants 93:24; see also Jacob 4:13.
6. Russell M. Nelson, "Revelation for the Church, Revelation for Our Lives," *Ensign* or *Liahona*, May 2018, 95.

7. "Zion, in process of time, was taken up into heaven" (Moses 7:21).
8. Psalm 30:5.
9. "How Gentle God's Commands," *Hymns*, no. 125; see also Psalm 55:22: "Cast thy burden upon the Lord, and he shall sustain thee," which is quoted in "Cast Thy Burden upon the Lord," *Hymns*, no. 110.
10. "Come, Ye Disconsolate," *Hymns*, no. 115.
11. See Alma 5:13.
12. See Mosiah 3:19.
13. See Doctrine and Covenants 58:42–43.
14. See Doctrine and Covenants 64:10.
15. Matthew 10:16; see also Alma 18:22.
16. See 3 Nephi 9:20.
17. John 3:17.
18. Romans 8:35, 38–39.
19. Isaiah 59:2.
20. Alma 34:10.
21. Luke 15:20.
22. The finest robe, ring, shoes, even the fatted calf, as it were (see Luke 15:22–23).
23. J. Reuben Clark Jr., in Conference Report, Oct. 1953, 84.
24. Luke 23:34; see also Matthew 6:12—"Forgive us our debts, as we forgive our debtors"—which also relates our ability to be forgiven to our willingness to forgive.
25. See Luke 15:11–32.
26. Luke 15:29.
27. We can receive the blessings of "the power of godliness" through restored ordinances and covenants, as Doctrine and Covenants 84:20 teaches.
28. Mark 5:36; see also Luke 8:50.
29. See "Joseph Smith's First Prayer," *Hymns*, no. 26.

GIVING HOLINESS TO THE LORD

BISHOP L. TODD BUDGE
Second Counselor in the Presiding Bishopric

Last year, while serving in the Asia North Area Presidency, I received a phone call from President Russell M. Nelson inviting me to serve as the Second Counselor in the Presiding Bishopric. He graciously invited my wife, Lori, to join the conversation. After the call was finished, we were still in a state of disbelief when my wife asked, "What does the Presiding Bishopric do anyway?" After a moment's reflection, I responded, "I don't know exactly!"

A year later—and after profound feelings of humility and gratitude—I can answer my wife's question with greater understanding. Among many other things, the Presiding Bishopric oversees the welfare and humanitarian work of the Church. This work now spans the entire globe and blesses more of God's children than ever before.

As a Presiding Bishopric, we are assisted by wonderful Church employees and others, including the Relief Society General Presidency, who serve with us on the Church's Welfare and Self-Reliance Executive Committee. In our capacity as members of that committee, the First Presidency asked me—as well as Sister Sharon Eubank, who spoke to us last evening—to share with you an update on the Church's recent humanitarian efforts. They also particularly requested that we express their profound gratitude—because, brothers and sisters, it is you who have made those humanitarian efforts possible.

As we observed with concern the early economic effects of the COVID-19 crisis across the world, we could have easily expected a decline in the monetary contributions which the Saints were able to give. After all, our own members were not immune to the setbacks from the pandemic. Imagine our feelings when we observed just the opposite! Humanitarian donations in 2020 turned out to be the highest ever—and are trending even higher this year. As a result of your generosity, the Church has been able to realize its most extensive response since the inception of the Humanitarian Fund, with over 1,500 COVID relief projects in more than 150 countries. These donations, which you have given so selflessly to the Lord, have been converted to life-sustaining food, oxygen, medical supplies, and vaccinations for those who might otherwise have gone without.

Just as significant as the contribution of goods is the tremendous outpouring of time and energy which Church members donate to humanitarian causes. Even as the pandemic has raged, natural disasters, civil conflict, and economic instability have been unrelenting and have continued to drive millions of people from their homes. The United Nations now reports that there are over 82 million forcibly displaced people in the world.[1] Add to this the millions of others who elect to flee from poverty or oppression in search of a better life for themselves or their children, and you can begin to catch a glimpse of the magnitude of this global situation.

I am pleased to report that thanks to the volunteer time and talents of so many, the Church operates refugee and immigrant welcome centers in multiple locations in the United States and Europe. And thanks to your contributions, we provide goods, funding, and volunteers to help similar programs run by other organizations throughout the world.

May I extend my heartfelt gratitude to those Saints who have reached out to feed, clothe, and befriend these refugees and help them become established and self-sufficient.

Yesterday evening, Sister Eubank shared with you a few of the Saints' wonderful efforts in this regard. As I reflect on these efforts, my thoughts often turn to the principle of sacrifice and the direct connection of this principle to the two great commandments of loving God and loving our neighbor.

In modern usage, the term *sacrifice* has come to connote the concept of "giving up" things for the Lord and His kingdom. However, in ancient days, the meaning of the word *sacrifice* was more closely tied to its two Latin roots: *sacer*, meaning "sacred" or "holy," and *facere*, meaning "to make."[2] Thus, anciently *sacrifice* meant literally "to make something or someone holy."[3] Viewed as such, sacrifice is a process of becoming holy and coming to know God, not an event or ritualistic "giving up" of things for the Lord.

The Lord said, "I desired [charity], and not sacrifice; and the knowledge of God more than burnt offerings."[4] The Lord wants us to become holy,[5] to be possessed of charity,[6] and to come to know Him.[7] As the Apostle Paul taught, "And though I bestow all my goods to feed the poor, and though I give my body to be burned, and have not charity, it profiteth me nothing."[8] Ultimately, the Lord wants our hearts; He wants us to become new creatures in Christ.[9] As He instructed the Nephites, "Ye shall offer for a sacrifice *unto* me a broken heart and a contrite spirit."[10]

Sacrifice is less about "giving *up*" and more about "giving *to*" the Lord. Engraved upon the entrance to each of our temples are the words "Holiness to the Lord; the House of the Lord." As we observe our covenants by sacrifice, we are made holy through the grace of Jesus Christ; and at the altars of the holy temple, with broken hearts and contrite spirits, we give our holiness to the Lord. Elder Neal A. Maxwell taught: "The submission of one's will [or heart[11]] is really the only uniquely personal thing we have to place on God's altar. . . . However, when you and I finally submit ourselves, by letting our individual wills be swallowed up in God's will, then we are really giving something *to* Him!"[12]

When our sacrifices on behalf of others are viewed from the perspective of "giving up," we may see them as a burden and become discouraged when our sacrifices are not recognized or rewarded. However, when viewed from the perspective of "giving to" the Lord, our sacrifices on behalf of others become gifts, and the joy of generously giving becomes its own reward. Freed from the need for love, approval, or appreciation from others, our sacrifices become the purest and deepest expressions of our gratitude and love for the Savior and our fellow men. Any prideful sense of self-sacrifice gives way to feelings of gratitude, generosity, contentment, and joy.[13]

Something is made holy—whether it be our lives, our possessions, our time, or our talents—not simply by giving it up but rather by consecrating[14] it to the Lord. The humanitarian work of the Church is such a gift. It is the product of the collective, consecrated offerings of the Saints, a manifestation of our love for God and His children.[15]

Steve and Anita Canfield are representative of Latter-day Saints throughout the world who have experienced for themselves the transformative blessings of giving to the Lord. As welfare and self-reliance missionaries, the Canfields were asked to provide aid at refugee camps and immigrant centers across Europe. In her professional life, Sister Canfield had been a world-class interior designer, contracted by wealthy clients to beautify their luxury homes. Suddenly she found herself thrust into a world that was the complete opposite, as she served among people who had lost nearly everything in terms of earthly possessions. In her words, she exchanged "marble walkways for dirt floors," and in doing so she found an immeasurable degree of fulfillment, as she and her husband began to befriend—and soon to love and embrace—those who needed their care.

The Canfields observed, "We did not feel as though we had 'given up' anything to serve the Lord. Our desire was simply to 'give to' Him our time and energies to bless His children in whatever way He saw fit to use us. As we worked alongside our brothers and sisters, any outward appearances—any differences in backgrounds or belongings—dissolved for us, and we simply saw one another's hearts. There is no degree of career success or material gains that could have equaled the way that these experiences, serving among the humblest of God's children, enriched us."

The Canfields' story and so many others like it have helped me appreciate the lyrics of a simple yet profound Primary song:

> *"Give," said the little stream,*
> *As it hurried down the hill;*
> *"I'm small, I know, but wherever I go*
> *The fields grow greener still."*

Yes, each of us is small, but together, as we hasten to give to God and our fellow men, wherever we go lives are enriched and blessed.

The third verse of this song is less well known but concludes with this loving invitation:

> *Give, then, as Jesus gives;*
> *There is something all can give.*
> *Do as the streams and blossoms do:*
> *For God and others live.*[16]

Dear brothers and sisters, as we live for God and others by giving of our means, our time, and yes, even of ourselves, we are leaving the world a little greener, leaving God's children a little happier, and in the process, becoming a little holier.

May the Lord bless you richly for the sacrifices that you give *to* Him so freely.

I testify that God lives. "Man of Holiness is his name."[17] Jesus Christ is His Son, and He is the giver of all good gifts.[18] May we, through His grace and the observance of our covenants by sacrifice, be made holy and ever give more love and holiness to the Lord.[19] In the holy name of Jesus Christ, amen.

Notes

1. See "Global Trends: Forced Displacement in 2020," UNHCR report, June 18, 2021, unhcr.org.
2. *Sacrifice* is derived from the Latin *sacrificium*, which is comprised of the two Latin roots *sacer* and *facere*, according to the *Merriam-Webster Dictionary* (see merriam-webster.com). The word *sacer* means "sacred" or "holy," and the word *facere* means "to make or do," according to the *Latin-English Dictionary* (see latin-english.com).
3. Guide to the Scriptures, "Sacrifice," scriptures.ChurchofJesusChrist.org.
4. Hosea 6:6; see footnote *b*, indicating that *mercy* in Hebrew means "charity" or "lovingkindness." See also Matthew 9:10–13; 12:7.
5. See Leviticus 11:44.
6. See Moroni 7:47.
7. See Mosiah 5:13.
8. 1 Corinthians 13:3; see also Mosiah 2:21.
9. See 2 Corinthians 5:17.
10. 3 Nephi 9:20, emphasis added; see also verse 19.
11. The word *heart* is added here as a synonym for *will*.
12. Neal A. Maxwell, "Swallowed Up in the Will of the Father," *Ensign*, Nov. 1995, 24; emphasis added. See also Omni 1:26; Romans 12:1.
13. See Moroni 10:3.
14. *Consecrate* means to "declare or set apart as sacred," according to the *American Heritage Dictionary*.
15. See Matthew 22:36–40.
16. "'Give,' Said the Little Stream," *Children's Songbook*, 236.
17. Moses 6:57.
18. See Moroni 10:18.
19. See Doctrine and Covenants 97:8.

REMEMBER THY SUFFERING SAINTS, O OUR GOD

ELDER ANTHONY D. PERKINS
Of the Seventy

Heavenly Father's plan of happiness includes a mortal experience where all of His children will be tested and face trials.[1] Five years ago I was diagnosed with cancer. I have felt and still feel the physical pains from surgeries, radiation treatments, and medication side effects. I have experienced emotional struggles during torturous sleepless nights. Medical statistics indicate I will probably depart mortality earlier than I ever expected, leaving behind, for a season, a family who means everything to me.

Regardless of where you live, physical or emotional suffering from a variety of trials and mortal weaknesses has been, is now, or will someday be part of your life.

Physical suffering can result from natural aging, unexpected diseases, and random accidents; hunger or homelessness; or abuse, violent acts, and war.

Emotional suffering can arise from anxiety or depression; the betrayal of a spouse, parent, or trusted leader; employment or financial reversals; unfair judgment by others; the choices of friends, children, or other family members; abuse in its many forms; unfulfilled dreams of marriage or children; the severe illness or early death of loved ones; or so many other sources.

How can you possibly endure the unique and sometimes debilitating suffering that comes to each of us?

Gratefully, hope is found in the gospel of Jesus Christ, and hope can also be part of your life. Today I share four principles of hope drawn from scripture, prophetic teachings, many ministering visits, and my own ongoing health trial. These principles are not just broadly applicable but also deeply personal.

First, suffering does not mean God is displeased with your life. Two thousand years ago, Jesus's disciples saw a blind man at the temple and asked, "Master, who did sin, this man, or his parents, that he was born blind?"

His disciples seemed to incorrectly believe, as do far too many people today, that all hardship and suffering in life are the result of sin. But the Savior replied, "Neither hath this man sinned, nor his parents: but that the works of God should be made manifest in him."[2]

The work of God is to bring to pass our immortality and eternal life.[3] But how can trials and suffering—especially suffering imposed by another person's sinful use of agency[4]—ultimately advance God's work?

The Lord told His covenant people, "I have refined thee . . . ; I have chosen thee in the furnace of affliction."[5] Whatever the cause of your sufferings, your loving Heavenly Father can direct them to refine your soul.[6] Refined souls can bear others' burdens with true empathy and compassion.[7] Refined souls who have come "out of great tribulation" are prepared to joyfully live in God's presence forever, and "God shall wipe away all tears from their eyes."[8]

Second, Heavenly Father is intimately aware of your suffering. While in the midst of trials, we can mistakenly think that God is far away and unconcerned with our pain. Even the Prophet Joseph Smith expressed this feeling at a low point in his life. When imprisoned in Liberty Jail while thousands of Latter-day Saints were being driven from their homes, Joseph sought understanding through prayer: "O God, where art thou? And where is the pavilion that covereth thy hiding place?" He ended with this plea: "Remember thy suffering saints, O our God."[9]

The Lord's answer reassured Joseph and all who suffer:

"My son, peace be unto thy soul; thine adversity and thine afflictions shall be but a small moment;

"And then, if thou endure it well, God shall exalt thee on high."[10]

Many suffering Saints have shared with me how they felt God's love during their trials. I vividly recall my own experience at one point in my cancer battle when the doctors had not yet diagnosed the cause of some severe pain. I sat with my wife, intending to offer a routine blessing on our lunch. Instead, all I could do was simply weep, "Heavenly Father, please help me. I am so sick." For the next 20 to 30 seconds, I was encircled in His love. I was given no reason for my illness, no indication of the ultimate outcome, and no relief from the pain. I just felt of His pure love, and that was and is enough.

I witness that our Heavenly Father, who notes the fall of even a single sparrow, is aware of your suffering.[11]

Third, Jesus Christ offers His enabling power to help you have strength to endure your suffering well. This enabling power is made possible through His Atonement.[12] I fear that too many Church members think if they are just a little tougher, they can get through any suffering on their own. This is a hard way to live. Your temporary moment of strength can never compare to the Savior's infinite supply of power to fortify your soul.[13]

The Book of Mormon teaches that Jesus Christ would "take upon him" our pains, sicknesses, and infirmities so He can succor us.[14] How can you draw upon the power that Jesus Christ offers to succor you and strengthen you in times of suffering? The key is binding yourself to the Savior by keeping the covenants you have made with Him. We make these covenants as we receive priesthood ordinances.[15]

The people of Alma entered into the covenant of baptism. Later they suffered in bondage and were forbidden to worship publicly or even pray aloud. Yet they kept their covenants the best they could by crying out silently in their hearts. As a result, divine power came. "The Lord did strengthen them that they could bear up their burdens with ease."[16]

In our day, the Savior invites, "Look unto me in every thought; doubt not, fear not."[17] When we keep our sacrament covenant to always remember Him, He promises that His Spirit will be with us. The Spirit gives us strength to endure trials and do what we cannot possibly do on our own. The Spirit can heal us, although as President James E. Faust taught, "Some of the healing may take place in another world."[18]

We are also blessed by temple covenants and ordinances, where "the power of godliness is manifest."[19] I visited a woman who had lost a teenage daughter in a terrible accident, then later her husband to cancer. I asked how she could endure such loss and suffering. She replied that strength came from spiritual reassurances of an eternal family, received during regular temple worship. As promised, the ordinances of the Lord's house had armed her with God's power.[20]

Fourth, choose to find joy each day. Those who suffer often feel that the night just goes on and on, and daylight will never come. It is OK to weep.[21] Yet, if you find yourself in dark nights of suffering, by choosing faith you can awake to bright mornings of rejoicing.[22]

For example, I visited a young mother being treated for cancer, smiling majestically in her chair despite the pain and a lack of hair. I met a middle-aged couple happily serving as youth leaders though they were unable to conceive children. I sat with a dear woman—a young grandmother, mother, and wife—who would pass away within days, yet amid the family's tears were laughter and joyful recollections.

These suffering Saints exemplify what President Russell M. Nelson has taught:

"The joy we feel has little to do with the circumstances of our lives and everything to do with the focus of our lives.

"When the focus of our lives is on God's plan of salvation . . . and Jesus Christ and His gospel, we can feel joy regardless of what is happening—or not happening—in our lives."[23]

I testify[24] that our Heavenly Father remembers His suffering Saints, loves you, and is intimately aware of you. Our Savior knows how you feel. "Surely he has borne our griefs, and carried our sorrows."[25] I know—as a daily recipient[26]—that keeping covenants unlocks the power of Jesus Christ's atoning sacrifice to provide strength and even joy to you who suffer.

For all who suffer, I pray, "May God grant unto you that your burdens may be light, through the joy of his Son."[27] In the name of Jesus Christ, amen.

Notes

1. See 1 Peter 4:12–13.
2. See John 9:1–3.
3. See Moses 1:39.
4. Sinful uses of agency that cause suffering to others are too many to list but surely include a spouse who commits adultery, a person who abuses a child or an adult, a drunk driver who injures or kills a loved one, or a mass shooter or a terrorist bomber who maims or kills many.
5. Isaiah 48:10; see also Zechariah 13:9.
6. See 2 Nephi 2:1–2.
7. Elder Robert D. Hales taught: "We must develop the ability to have a concern for others while we are suffering. It is a key element in our spiritual growth. As we lose our lives in the service of our fellowmen, we find ourselves" ("Your Sorrow Shall Be Turned to Joy," *Ensign*, Nov. 1983, 66).
8. See Revelation 7:13–17; 21:3–4.
9. Doctrine and Covenants 121:1, 6.
10. Doctrine and Covenants 121:7–8.
11. See Matthew 10:29–31.
12. See Bible Dictionary, "Grace."
13. See Philippians 4:13, 19; Alma 26:12; see also 2 Chronicles 32:7–8.
14. See Alma 7:11–13; see also 2 Nephi 9:21.
15. See *General Handbook: Serving in The Church of Jesus Christ of Latter-day Saints*, 3.5, ChurchofJesusChrist.org.
16. See Mosiah 24:13–15.
17. Doctrine and Covenants 6:36.
18. James E. Faust, "Where Do I Make My Stand?," *Ensign* or *Liahona*, Nov. 2004, 21.
19. Doctrine and Covenants 84:20.
20. See Doctrine and Covenants 109:22; see also 1 Nephi 14:14.
21. See John 11:35; Doctrine and Covenants 42:45.
22. This idea is inspired by Elder Joseph B. Wirthlin's message "Sunday Will Come," *Ensign* or *Liahona*, Nov. 2006, 28–30. See also James 1:2–4 (including the Joseph Smith Translation in footnote 2a); 5:10–11.
23. Russell M. Nelson, "Joy and Spiritual Survival," *Ensign* or *Liahona*, Nov. 2016, 82.
24. Twenty years ago, the Apostle Elder Neal A. Maxwell was pondering his painful and ultimately life-ending illness. The Spirit whispered, "I have given you leukemia that you might teach my people with authenticity" (see Bruce C. Hafen, *A Disciple's Life: The Biography of Neal A. Maxwell* [2002], 562).
25. Mosiah 14:4; see also Isaiah 53:4.
26. The more appropriate scriptural word for *recipient* is *partaker* (see Ether 12:6–9).
27. Alma 33:23.

ONE PERCENT BETTER

ELDER MICHAEL A. DUNN

Of the Seventy

For more than a century, the national bicycle racing teams of Great Britain had been the laughingstock of the cycling world. Mired in mediocrity, British riders had managed only a handful of gold medals in 100 years of Olympic competitions and had been even more underwhelming in cycling's marquee event, the three-week long Tour de France—where no British rider had prevailed in 110 years. So sorry was the plight of British riders that some bike manufacturers refused to even sell bikes to the Brits, fearing it would forever sully their hard-won reputations. And despite devoting enormous resources into cutting-edge technology and every newfangled training regimen, nothing worked.

Nothing, that is, until 2003, when a small, largely unnoticed change occurred that would forever alter the trajectory of British cycling. That new approach would also reveal an eternal principle—with a promise—regarding our ofttimes perplexing mortal quest to improve ourselves. So what happened in British cycling that has great relevance to our personal pursuit to be better daughters and sons of God?

In 2003, Sir Dave Brailsford was hired. Unlike previous coaches who attempted dramatic, overnight turnarounds, Sir Brailsford instead committed to a strategy he referred to as "the aggregation of marginal gains." This entailed implementing small improvements in everything. That meant constantly measuring key statistics and targeting specific weaknesses.

It's somewhat akin to the prophet Samuel the Lamanite's notion of "walk[ing] circumspectly."[1] This broader, more holistic view avoids the trap of being myopically fixated on just the obvious problem or sin at hand. Said Brailsford, "The whole principle came from the idea that if you broke down everything you could think of that goes into riding a bike, and then improved it by 1 percent, you will get a significant increase when you put them all together."[2]

His approach aligns well with that of the Lord, who taught us the criticalness of the 1 percent—even at the expense of the 99 percent. Of course, He was teaching the gospel imperative to seek out individuals in need. But what if we applied that same principle to the very sweet and savory second principle of the gospel, repentance? Rather than being stymied by the churn and dramatic swings between sin and repentance, what if our approach was to narrow our focus—even as we broadened it? Instead of trying to perfect everything, what if we tackled just one thing?

For example, what if in your new wide-angle awareness, you discover you have neglected a daily reading of the Book of Mormon? Well, instead of desperately plowing through all 531 pages in one night, what if we committed instead to read just 1 percent of it—that's just five pages a day—or another manageable goal for your situation? Could aggregating small but steady *marginal gains* in our lives finally be the way to victory over even the most pesky of our personal shortcomings? Can this bite-sized approach to tackling our blemishes really work?

Well, acclaimed author James Clear says this strategy puts the math squarely in our favor. He maintains that "habits are the 'compound interest of self-improvement.' If you can get just one percent better at something each day, by the end of a year . . . you will be 37 times better."[3]

Brailsford's small gains began with the obvious, such as equipment, kit fabrics, and training patterns. But his team didn't stop there. They continued to find 1 percent improvements in overlooked and unexpected areas such as nutrition and even maintenance nuances. Over time, these myriads of micro-betterments aggregated into stunning results, which came faster than anyone could have imagined. Truly, they were onto the eternal principle of "line upon line, precept upon precept, here a little and there a little."[4]

Will little adjustments work that "mighty change"[5] that you desire? Properly implemented, I'm 99 percent certain they will! But the one caveat with this approach is that for small gains to aggregate, there must be a consistent, day-in and day-out effort. And although we won't likely be perfect, we must be determined to mirror our persistence with patience. Do that, and the sweet rewards of increased righteousness will bring you the joy and peace you seek. As President Russell M. Nelson has taught: "Nothing is more liberating, more ennobling, or more crucial to our individual progression than is a regular, daily focus on repentance. Repentance is not an event; it is a process. It is the key to happiness and peace of mind. When coupled with faith, repentance opens our access to the power of the Atonement of Jesus Christ."[6]

As to repentance's prerequisite of faith, the scriptures are clear. All that's initially required is a mere "particle of faith."[7] And if we can muster this "mustard seed"[8] mentality, we too can expect unexpected and exceptional improvements in our lives. But remember, just as we would not attempt to go from being Attila the Hun to Mother Teresa overnight, so too should we reorient our patterns of improvement incrementally. Even if the changes needed in your life are wholesale, begin at a small scale. That's especially true if you are feeling overwhelmed or discouraged.

This process is not always accomplished in a linear fashion. Even among the most determined there may be setbacks. Having experienced the frustration of this in my own life, I know that it can sometimes feel like 1 percent forward and 2 percent back. Yet if we remain undaunted in our determination to consistently eke out those 1 percent gains, He who has "carried our sorrows"[9] will surely carry us.

Obviously, if we are involved in grievous sins, the Lord is clear and unequivocal; we need to stop, get help from our bishop, and turn away from such practices immediately. But as Elder David A. Bednar enjoined: "Small, steady, incremental spiritual improvements are the steps the Lord would have us take. Preparing to walk guiltless before God is one of the primary purposes of mortality and the pursuit of a lifetime; it does not result from sporadic spurts of intense spiritual activity."[10]

So, does this pocket-sized approach to repentance and real change really work? Is the proof in the pedaling, so to speak?

Consider what's happened to British cycling in the past two decades since implementing this philosophy. British cyclists have now won the storied Tour de France an astonishing six times. During the past four Olympic Games, Great Britain has been the most successful country across all cycling disciplines. And in the recently concluded Tokyo Olympics, the UK won more gold medals in cycling than any other country.

But far outshining worldly silver or gold, our precious promise down our roadway to the eternities is that we will indeed "triumph in Christ."[11] And as we commit to making small but steady improvements, we are promised "a crown of glory that fadeth not away."[12] With basking in that undimmable luster beckoning, I invite you to examine your life and see what's stagnated or slowed you on the covenant pathway. Then look broader. Seek modest but makeable fixes in your life that might result in the sweet joy of being just a little better.

Remember, David used just one small stone to take down a seemingly invincible giant. But he had four other stones at the ready. Similarly, Alma the Younger's wicked disposition and eternal destiny were altered by just one simple, salient thought—a remembrance of his father's teachings about the saving grace of Jesus Christ. And so it is with our Savior, who, though sinless, "received not of the fulness at first, but continued from grace to grace, until he received a fulness."[13]

It is He who knows when a sparrow falls that is likewise focused on the minute as well as the momentous moments in our lives and who is ready right now to assist you in whatever your 1 percent quest is coming out of this conference. Because every effort to change we make—no matter how tiny it seems to us—just might make the biggest difference in our lives.

To this end, Elder Neal A. Maxwell taught, "Each assertion of a righteous desire, each act of service, and each act of worship, however small and incremental, adds to our spiritual momentum."[14] Truly, it is by small, simple, and, yes, even just 1 percent things that great things can be brought to pass.[15] Ultimate victory is 100 percent certain, "after all we can do,"[16] through the might, merits, and mercy of our Lord and Savior, Jesus Christ. I so testify in the name of Jesus Christ, amen.

Notes

1. Helaman 15:5.
2. See James Clear, "This Coach Improved Every Tiny Thing by 1 Percent and Here's What Happened," jamesclear.com/marginal-gains.
3. James Clear, in Whitney Johnson, "James Clear: Just One Percent Better," whitneyjohnson .com/james-clear.
4. 2 Nephi 28:30.
5. Alma 5:14.
6. Russell M. Nelson, "We Can Do Better and Be Better," *Ensign* or *Liahona*, May 2019, 67.
7. Alma 32:27.
8. Matthew 17:20.
9. Isaiah 53:4.
10. David A. Bednar, "Clean Hands and a Pure Heart," *Ensign* or *Liahona*, Nov. 2007, 82.
11. 2 Corinthians 2:14.
12. 1 Peter 5:4.
13. Doctrine and Covenants 93:13.
14. Neal A. Maxwell, "According to the Desire of [Our] Hearts," *Ensign*, Nov. 1996, 22.
15. See Alma 37:6.
16. 2 Nephi 25:23.

FACING OUR SPIRITUAL HURRICANES BY BELIEVING IN CHRIST

ELDER SEAN DOUGLAS
Of the Seventy

For the past six years, my sweetheart, Ann, and I have lived in Texas near the Gulf Coast, where some of the largest hurricanes have struck the United States, leaving behind tremendous destruction and even loss of life. Sadly enough, recent months have been no stranger to such devastating events. Our love and prayers extend to all who have been impacted in any way. In 2017 we personally experienced Hurricane Harvey, which dropped record rainfall of up to 60 inches (150 cm).

Natural laws govern the formation of hurricanes. The ocean temperature must be at least 80 degrees Fahrenheit (27 degrees C), extending to 165 feet (50 m) below the ocean's surface. As wind meets the warm ocean water, it causes the water to vaporize and rise into the atmosphere, where it liquifies. Clouds then form, and winds produce a spiral pattern over the ocean's surface.

Hurricanes are colossal in size, reaching 50,000 feet (15,240 m) or more into the atmosphere and spanning at least 125 miles (200 km) across. Interestingly, as hurricanes meet land, they begin to weaken because they are no longer above the warm waters required to fuel their strength.[1]

You may never face a devastating physical hurricane. However, each of us has weathered and will weather spiritual hurricanes that threaten our peace and try our faith. In today's world, they seem to be increasing in frequency and intensity. Thankfully, the Lord has provided us a sure way to joyfully overcome them. By living the gospel of Jesus Christ, we are assured that "when dark clouds of trouble hang o'er us and threaten our peace to destroy, there is hope smiling brightly before us."[2]

President Russell M. Nelson explained:

"Saints can be happy under every circumstance. We can feel joy even while having a bad day, a bad week, or even a bad year!

". . . The joy we feel has little to do with the circumstances of our lives and everything to do with the focus of our lives.

"When the focus of our lives is on . . . Jesus Christ and His gospel, we can feel joy regardless of what is happening—or not happening—in our lives."[3]

Just as natural laws govern physical hurricanes, divine laws govern how to feel joy during our spiritual hurricanes. The joy or misery we feel as we brave the storms of life is tied to the laws that God has set. President Nelson has shared, "They're called commandments, but they are just as true as the law of lift, the law of gravity, [and] the law that governs the heartbeat."

President Nelson continued, "It becomes a rather simple formula: If you want to be happy, keep the commandments."[4]

Doubt is an enemy of faith and joy. Just as warm ocean water is the breeding ground for hurricanes, doubt is the breeding ground for spiritual hurricanes. Just as belief is a choice, so is doubt. When we choose to doubt, we choose to be acted upon, yielding power to the adversary, thereby leaving us weak and vulnerable.[5]

Satan seeks to lead us to the breeding ground of doubt. He seeks to harden our hearts so that we will not believe.[6] The breeding ground of doubt can appear inviting because its seemingly peaceful, warm waters do not require us to "live by every word that proceedeth forth from the mouth of God."[7] In such waters Satan tempts us to relax our spiritual vigilance. That inattention can induce a lack of spiritual conviction, where we are "neither cold nor hot."[8] If we are not anchored on Christ, doubt and its allures will lead us away to apathy, where we shall find neither miracles, lasting happiness, nor "rest unto [our] souls."[9]

Just as hurricanes weaken over land, doubt is replaced with faith as we build our foundation on Christ. We are then able to see spiritual hurricanes in their proper perspective, and our capacity to overcome them is enlarged. Then, "when the devil shall send forth his mighty winds, yea, his shafts in the whirlwind, . . . it shall have no power . . . to drag [us] down to the gulf of misery and endless wo, because of the rock upon which [we] are built, which is a sure foundation."[10]

President Nelson has taught:

"Faith in Jesus Christ is the foundation of all belief and the conduit of divine power. . . .

"The Lord does not require *perfect* faith for us to have access to His *perfect* power. But He does ask us to believe."[11]

Since April general conference, my family and I have been seeking to strengthen our faith in Jesus Christ and His Atonement to help us "turn [our] challenges into unparalleled growth and opportunity."[12]

Our granddaughter Ruby has been blessed with a strong, take-charge will. When she was born, her esophagus was not attached to her stomach. Even as an infant, Ruby, with her parents' help, met this trial with unusual determination. Ruby is now five years old. Though she is still very young, she is a powerful example of not letting her circumstances determine her happiness. She is always happy.

Last May, Ruby faced an additional hurricane in her life with faith. She was also born with less than a fully developed hand that needed reconstructive surgery. Prior to this rather complex operation, we visited with her and gave her a drawing that beautifully depicts a child's hand warmly holding the hand of the Savior. When we asked her if she was nervous, she replied, "No, I am happy!"

Then we asked her, "Ruby, how is that so?"

Ruby confidently asserted, "Because I know that Jesus will hold my hand."

Ruby's recovery has been miraculous, and she continues to be happy. How the purity of a child's faith contrasts with the foolishness of doubt that can frequently tempt us as we get older![13] But we can all become as little children and choose to put aside our unbelief. It is a simple choice.

A caring father diligently pleaded with the Savior, saying, "If thou canst do any thing, . . . help us."[14]

Jesus then said unto him:

"If thou canst believe, all things are possible to him that believeth.

"And straightway the father . . . cried out, and said with tears, Lord, I believe; help thou mine unbelief."[15]

This humble father wisely chose to trust his belief in Christ rather than his doubt. President Nelson shared, "Only *your* unbelief will keep God from blessing you with miracles to move the mountains in *your* life."[16]

How merciful is our God to place the bar for us at the level of believing and not at the level of knowing!

Alma teaches:

"Blessed is he that believeth in the word of God."[17]

"[For] God is merciful unto all who believe on his name; therefore he desireth, in the first place, that ye should believe."[18]

Yes, in the first place, God desires that we believe in Him.

We face our spiritual hurricanes best by believing in Christ and keeping His commandments. Our belief and obedience link us to power beyond our own to overcome "[whatever] is happening—or not happening—in our lives."[19] Yes, God "doth immediately bless [us]" for believing and obeying.[20] In fact, over time our state of being changes to happiness, and "we are made alive in Christ" as we exercise our faith in Him and keep His commandments.[21]

Brothers and sisters, may we choose today to "doubt not, but be believing."[22] "The right way is to believe in Christ."[23] We are "graven . . . upon the palms of [His] hands."[24] He is our Savior and Redeemer, who stands at our very door and knocks.[25] In the name of Jesus Christ, amen.

Notes

1. See Lee Cook, "What Weather Conditions Create a Hurricane," July 29, 2019, Sciencing, sciencing.com.
2. "We Thank Thee, O God, for a Prophet," *Hymns*, no. 19.
3. Russell M. Nelson, "Joy and Spiritual Survival," *Ensign* or *Liahona*, Nov. 2016, 82.
4. Russell M. Nelson, in "Eternal Laws: From Scrabble to the Commandments" (video), *Church News*, Aug. 31, 2019, thechurchnews.com; see also Mosiah 2:41; Doctrine and Covenants 130:20–21.
5. See 2 Nephi 2:26–27.
6. See Doctrine and Covenants 10:32–33.

7. Doctrine and Covenants 84:44; see also Deuteronomy 8:3; Matthew 4:4; Doctrine and Covenants 98:11.
8. Revelation 3:15–16.
9. See 2 Nephi 28:21–26. In contrast, see Matthew 11:28–30 and note the "rest" Christ will give us as we come unto Him.
10. Helaman 5:12.
11. Russell M. Nelson, "Christ Is Risen; Faith in Him Will Move Mountains," *Liahona*, May 2021, 102.
12. Russell M. Nelson, "Christ Is Risen; Faith in Him Will Move Mountains," 104.
13. See 2 Nephi 9:28–29.
14. Mark 9:22. Note the father pleaded for Christ to help "us"—parents and child together, seeking the Savior's love and healing power.
15. Mark 9:23–24.
16. Russell M. Nelson, "Christ Is Risen; Faith in Him Will Move Mountains," 103.
17. Alma 32:16. The full verse reads, "Therefore, blessed are they who *humble* themselves without being *compelled* to be humble; or rather, in other words, blessed is he that believeth in the word of God, and is baptized without *stubbornness* of heart, yea, without being brought to know the word, or even compelled to know, before they will believe" (emphasis added). Note that the Lord desires that we believe without being compelled to be humble, without being stubborn, without being "brought" to know, and without being compelled to "know" before we will believe.
18. Alma 32:22.
19. Russell M. Nelson, "Joy and Spiritual Survival," 82.
20. Mosiah 2:24; see also Mosiah 2:41; Ether 12:4.
21. See 2 Nephi 25:24–25.
22. Mormon 9:27; see also 1 Nephi 4:3.
23. 2 Nephi 25:28.
24. 1 Nephi 21:16.
25. See Revelation 3:20. Note in verse 21 the promise made "to him that overcometh."

MIRACLES OF THE GOSPEL OF JESUS CHRIST

ELDER CARLOS G. REVILLO JR.
Of the Seventy

Mabuhay! I bring to you love and warm smiles from the wonderful Saints of the Philippines. This year marks 60 years since the first missionaries arrived in the islands of the Philippines. Today there are 23 missions and more than 800,000 members of the Church in 123 stakes. There are now seven temples in operation, under construction, or announced. This is truly a miracle. We are witnessing the fulfillment of the prophecy in 2 Nephi 10:21: "Great are the promises of the Lord unto them who are upon the isles of the sea."

This miracle is also a fulfillment of the prophecy given in a prayer by then-Elder Gordon B. Hinckley in Manila in 1961. In that prayer, Elder Hinckley stated: "We invoke Thy blessings upon the people of this land, that they shall be friendly and hospitable and kind and gracious to those who shall come here, and that many, yea, Lord, we pray that there shall be [many,] many thousands who shall receive this message and be blessed thereby. Wilt Thou bless them with receptive minds and understanding hearts, and with faith to receive, and with courage to live the principles of the gospel" (dedicatory prayer at American War Memorial Cemetery, Philippines, Apr. 28, 1961).

Beyond the many, many thousands of faithful Latter-day Saints, the miracle of the gospel has brought positive changes to the country and its people. I am a living witness of this. I was six years old when my parents joined the Church in the southern island of Mindanao. At that time, there was only one mission in the entire country and no stakes. I am eternally grateful for my parents' courage and commitment to follow the Savior. I honor them and all the pioneers of the Church in the Philippines. They paved the way for the succeeding generations to be blessed.

King Benjamin in the Book of Mormon said: "And moreover, I would desire that ye should consider on the blessed and happy state of those that keep the commandments of God. For behold, they are blessed in all things, both temporal and spiritual" (Mosiah 2:41).

As we live and obey the principles and ordinances of the gospel, we are blessed, changed, and converted to becoming more like Jesus Christ. That was how the gospel changed and blessed the Filipino Saints, including my family. The gospel is truly the way to a happy, abundant life.

The first principle of the gospel is faith in the Lord Jesus Christ. Many Filipinos have a natural belief in God. It is easy for us to trust Jesus Christ and know that we can receive answers to our prayers.

The Obedoza family is a great example of this. Brother Obedoza was my branch president when I was a young man. Brother and Sister Obedoza's greatest desire was to be sealed to their family in the Manila Temple. They lived in General Santos City, 1,000 miles (1,600 km) away from Manila. For the family of nine, making the journey to the temple seemed impossible. But like the merchant man who went and sold all he had to buy one pearl of great price (see Matthew 13:45–46), this couple decided to sell their house to pay for the trip. Sister Obedoza was worried because they would have no home to return to. But Brother Obedoza assured her that the Lord would provide.

They were sealed as a family for time and all eternity in the temple in 1985. In the temple they found joy incomparable—their priceless pearl. And true to Brother Obedoza's words, the Lord did provide. On their return from Manila, kind acquaintances gave them places to stay, and they eventually acquired their own home. The Lord takes care of those who demonstrate their faith in Him.

The second principle of the gospel is repentance. Repentance is turning away from sin and turning to God for forgiveness. It is a change of mind and heart. As President Russell M. Nelson teaches, it is "doing and being a little better each day" ("We Can Do Better and Be Better," *Ensign* or *Liahona*, May 2019, 67).

Repentance is a lot like soap. As a young chemical engineer, I worked in a soap factory in the Philippines. I learned how to make soap and the process of how it works. When you mix oils with an alkali base and add antibacterial agents, it creates a powerful substance that can eliminate bacteria and viruses. Like soap, repentance is a cleaning agent. It allows us the opportunity to get rid of our impurities and our old debris so we are worthy to be with God, as "no unclean thing can inherit the kingdom of [God]" (Alma 11:37).

Through repentance we draw upon the cleansing, sanctifying power of Jesus Christ. It is a key part of the process of conversion. This is what happened to the Anti-Nephi-Lehies in the Book of Mormon. They were Lamanites who were so completely converted that they "never did fall away" (see Alma 23:6–8). They buried their weapons of war and never took them up again. They would rather die than break that covenant. And they proved it. We know that their sacrifice brought miracles; thousands who fought against them threw down their weapons and were converted. Years later their sons, who we know as the mighty stripling warriors, were protected in battle against incredible odds!

My family and many Filipino Saints went through a similar conversion process. When we accepted the gospel of Jesus Christ and joined the Church, we changed our ways and our culture to align to the gospel. We had to let go of wrong traditions. I saw this in my father when he learned of the gospel and repented. He was a heavy smoker, but he threw his cigarettes away and never touched one again. Because of his decision to change, four generations from him have been blessed.

Repentance leads us to make and keep covenants through sacred ordinances. The first ordinance of salvation and exaltation is baptism by immersion for the remission of sins. Baptism allows us to receive the gift of the Holy Ghost and enter into a covenant with the Lord. We can renew this baptismal covenant every week as we take the sacrament. This too is a miracle!

Brothers and sisters, I invite you to bring this miracle into your life. Come unto Jesus Christ and choose to exercise your faith in Him; repent and make and keep the covenants found in the ordinances of salvation and exaltation. This will allow you to be yoked with Christ and receive the power and blessings of godliness (see Doctrine and Covenants 84:20).

I testify of the reality of Jesus Christ and that He lives and loves each one of us. I know that His gospel can bring us hope, peace, and joy, not only now, but it will also bless countless others in future generations. That is the reason for the beautiful and warm smiles of the Filipino Saints. It is the miracle of the gospel and the doctrine of Christ. I testify of this in the sacred name of Jesus Christ, amen.

LOOK DOWN THE ROAD

ELDER ALVIN F. MEREDITH III
Of the Seventy

When I turned 15 years old, I received a learner's permit, which allowed me to drive a car if one of my parents was with me. When my father asked if I would like to go for a drive, I was thrilled.

He drove a few miles to the outskirts of town to a long, straight, two-lane road that few people used—I should note, likely the only place he would have felt safe. He pulled over on the shoulder of the road, and we switched seats. He gave me some coaching and then told me, "Ease out onto the road and just drive until I tell you to stop."

I followed his orders exactly. But after about 60 seconds, he said, "Son, pull the car over. You're making me nauseous. You are swerving all over the road." He asked, "What are you looking at?"

With some exasperation, I said, "I'm looking at the road."

Then he said this: "I'm watching your eyes, and you are looking only at what is right in front of the hood of the car. If you look only at what is directly in front of you, you will never drive straight." Then he emphasized, "Look down the road. That will help you drive straight."

As a 15-year-old, I thought that was a good driving lesson. I have since realized that that was a great life lesson as well. Focusing on the things that are most important—especially those things "down the road," those eternal things—is a key to maneuvering through this life.

On one occasion in the Savior's life, He desired to be alone, so "he went up into a mountain apart to pray."[1] He sent His disciples away with instructions to cross the sea. In the dark of the night, the ship that carried the disciples came upon a ferocious storm. Jesus went to their rescue but in an unconventional way. The scripture account reads, "In the fourth watch of the night Jesus went unto them, walking on the sea."[2] When they saw Him, they began to fear, for they thought that the figure that approached them was some sort of ghost or phantom. Jesus, sensing their trepidation and wanting to put their minds and hearts at ease, called to them, "Be of good cheer; it is I; be not afraid."[3]

Peter was not only relieved but also emboldened. Ever courageous and often impetuous, Peter cried out to Jesus, "Lord, if it be thou, bid me come unto thee on the water."[4] Jesus replied with His familiar and timeless invitation: "Come."[5]

Peter, surely thrilled by the prospect, climbed out of the boat not into the water but onto the water. While he focused on the Savior, he could do the impossible, even walk on water. Initially, Peter was undeterred by the storm. But the "boisterous"[6] wind eventually distracted him, and he lost his focus. The fear returned. Consequently, his faith diminished, and he began to sink. "He cried, saying, Lord, save me."[7] The Savior, who is always eager to save, reached out and lifted him up to safety.

There are a myriad of lessons to learn from this miraculous account, but I will mention three.

Focus on Christ

The first lesson: focus on Jesus Christ. While Peter kept his eyes focused on Jesus, he could walk on water. The storm, the waves, and the wind could not hinder him as long he centered his focus on the Savior.

Understanding our ultimate purpose helps us determine what our focus should be. We cannot play a successful game without knowing the goal, nor can we live a meaningful life without knowing its purpose. One of the great blessings of the restored gospel of Jesus Christ is that it answers, among other things, the question "What is the purpose of life?" "Our purpose in this life is to have joy and prepare to return to God's presence."[8] Remembering that we are here on earth to prepare to return to live with God helps us focus on the things that lead us to Christ.

Focusing on Christ requires discipline, especially about the small and simple spiritual habits that help us become better disciples. There is no discipleship without discipline.

Our focus on Christ becomes more clear when we look down the road at where we want to be and who we want to become and then make time every day to do those things that will help us get there. Focusing on Christ can simplify our decisions and provide a guide for how we can best spend our time and resources.

While there are many things worthy of our focus, we learn from Peter's example the importance of always keeping Christ at the center of our focus. It is only through Christ that we can return to live with God. We rely on the grace of Christ as we strive to become like Him and seek His forgiveness and strengthening power when we fall short.

Beware of Distractions

The second lesson: beware of distractions. When Peter turned his focus away from Jesus and toward the wind and the waves that whipped at his feet, he began to sink.

There are many things "in front of the hood" that can distract us from focusing on Christ and eternal things that are "down the road." The devil is the great distractor. We learn from Lehi's dream that voices from the great and spacious building seek to lure us to things that will take us off the course of preparing to return to live with God.[9]

But there are other less-obvious distractions that can be just as dangerous. As the saying goes, "The only thing necessary for the triumph of evil is for good men to do nothing." The adversary seems determined to get good people to do nothing, or at least to waste their time on things that will distract them from their lofty purposes and goals. For example, some things that are healthy diversions in moderation can become unhealthy distractions without discipline. The adversary understands that distractions do not have to be bad or immoral to be effective.

We Can Be Rescued

The third lesson: we can be rescued. When Peter began to sink, he cried out, "Lord, save me. And immediately Jesus stretched forth his hand, and caught him."[10] When we find ourselves sinking, when we face affliction, or when we falter, we too can be rescued by Him.

In the face of affliction or trial, you may be like me and hope that the rescue will be immediate. But remember that the Savior came to the aid of the Apostles in the fourth watch of the night—after they had spent most of the night toiling in the storm.[11] We may pray that if the help will not come immediately, it will at least come in the second watch or even the third watch of the proverbial night. When we must wait, rest assured that the Savior is always watching, ensuring that we will not have to endure more than we can bear.[12] To those who are waiting in the fourth watch of the night, perhaps still in the midst of suffering, do not lose hope. Rescue always comes to the faithful, whether during mortality or in the eternities.

Sometimes our sinking comes because of our mistakes and transgressions. If you find yourself sinking for those reasons, make the joyful choice to repent.[13] I believe that few things give the Savior more joy than saving those who turn, or return, to Him.[14] The scriptures are full of stories of people who were once fallen and flawed but who repented and became firm in the faith of Christ. I think those stories are in the scriptures to remind us that the Savior's love for us and His power to redeem us are infinite. Not only does the Savior have joy when we repent, but we receive great joy as well.

Conclusion

I invite you to be intentional about "looking down the road" and increase your focus on those things that really matter. May we keep Christ at the center of our focus. In the midst of all the distractions, the things "in front of the hood," and the whirlwinds that surround us, I testify that Jesus is our Savior and our Redeemer and our Rescuer. In the name of Jesus Christ, amen.

Notes

1. Matthew 14:23.
2. Matthew 14:25.
3. Matthew 14:27.
4. Matthew 14:28.
5. Matthew 14:29.
6. Matthew 14:30.
7. Matthew 14:30.
8. *Preach My Gospel: A Guide to Missionary Service* (2019), 50.
9. See 1 Nephi 8:26–27; 12:18.
10. Matthew 14:30–31.
11. See Mark 6:48.
12. See 1 Corinthians 10:13.
13. See Dale G. Renlund, "Repentance: A Joyful Choice," *Ensign* or *Liahona*, Nov. 2016, 121–24.
14. See Doctrine and Covenants 18:13.

THE NAME OF THE CHURCH IS NOT NEGOTIABLE

ELDER NEIL L. ANDERSEN
Of the Quorum of the Twelve Apostles

In a press conference on August 16, 2018, President Russell M. Nelson said: "The Lord has impressed upon my mind the importance of the name He has revealed for His Church, even The Church of Jesus Christ of Latter-day Saints.[1] We have work before us to bring ourselves in harmony with His will."[2]

Two days later, on August 18, I was with President Nelson in Montreal, Canada. Following our member meeting in the impressive Palais de Congrés, President Nelson answered questions from reporters. He acknowledged that it was "going to be a challenge to [reestablish the name of the Church and] undo [a] tradition of more than a hundred years." But, he added, "the name of the Church is not negotiable."[3]

Seven weeks later, President Nelson spoke in general conference: "The Lord impressed upon my mind the importance of the name He decreed for His Church, even The Church of Jesus Christ of Latter-day Saints. . . . It was the Savior Himself who said, 'For thus shall my church be called.'" Then President Nelson repeated, "The name of the Church is not negotiable."[4]

A Good Question

A good question surfaced: Why now, when for many decades we had embraced the nickname "Mormon"? "The Mormon Tabernacle Choir," the video spots "I'm a Mormon," the Primary song "I Am a Mormon Boy"?

The doctrine of Christ is unchanging and everlasting. Yet specific and important steps of the Savior's work are revealed at their appropriate time. This morning President Nelson said, "The Restoration is a process, not an event."[5] And the Lord has said, "All things must come to pass in their time."[6] Now is our time, and we are reestablishing the revealed name of the Church.

The identity and destiny of The Church of Jesus Christ of Latter-day Saints require that we be called by His name. I was recently in Kirtland, Ohio, where the Prophet Joseph Smith, with only a few members of the Church, prophesied, "This Church will fill North and South America—it will fill the world."[7] The Lord described the work of this dispensation as "a marvelous work and a wonder."[8] He spoke of a "covenant [that would] be fulfilled in the latter days," allowing "all . . . the earth [to] be blessed."[9]

The words of this conference are being translated live into 55 languages. Eventually, these words will be heard and read in 98 languages in more than 220 countries and territories.

When the Savior returns in majesty and glory, faithful members of The Church of Jesus Christ of Latter-day Saints will be among all nations, all people, all races, and all cultures of the world.

The Growing Influence of the Church

The influence of the restored Church of Jesus Christ will not only be upon those who are members of the Church. Because of the heavenly manifestations in our day, because of the sacred scripture restored to the earth and the powerful gift of the Holy Ghost, we will be a shining light on the hill as the somber shades of disbelief in Jesus Christ darken the world. Although many may allow the world to cloud their faith in the Redeemer, we will "not be moved out of [our] place."[10] Christians who are not among our membership will welcome our role and our sure witness of Christ. Even those Christians who have viewed us with skepticism will embrace us as friends. In these coming days, we will be called by the name of Jesus Christ.

Thank you for your noble efforts to advance the true name of the Church. In the conference three years ago, President Nelson promised us "that our rigorous attention to use the correct name of the Savior's Church . . . [would bring us] increased faith and access to greater spiritual power."[11]

This promise has been realized by devoted disciples across the world.[12]

Brother Lauri Ahola from the eastern United States admits that at times he finds it awkward to share the full name of the Church. But because of the prophet's counsel, he persists. On one occasion, he was visiting a friend at a church of another faith. Here are his words:

An acquaintance asked, "Are you a Mormon?"

"'I am a member of The Church of Jesus Christ of Latter-day Saints, yes,' I said. He started asking me several questions, each beginning with: 'Does the Mormon Church believe . . . ?' And each time, I began my answer with the phrase: 'In the restored Church of [Jesus] Christ, we believe . . .'

". . . When he noticed that I wasn't accepting the title 'Mormon,' he asked me point-blank, 'Are you not Mormon?'

"So I asked him if he knew who Mormon was—he didn't. I told him that Mormon was a prophet . . . [and I was] honored to be associated with [him].

"'But,' I continued, 'Mormon didn't die for my sins. Mormon didn't . . . suffer in Gethsemane or die on the cross [for me]. . . . Jesus Christ is my God and my Savior. . . . And it is by His name that I want to be known. . . .'

". . . After a few seconds of silence, [the acquaintance exclaimed], 'So, you are a Christian!'"[13]

Remember President Nelson's words? "I promise you that if we will do our best to restore the correct name of the Lord's Church, He whose Church this is will pour down His power and blessings upon the heads of the Latter-day Saints, the likes of which we have never seen."[14]

The Lord Always Opens the Way

The Lord always keeps His promises. He opens the way for us as we do His work.

For years we had hoped to purchase the internet domain sites ChurchofJesusChrist.org and ChurchofJesusChrist.com. Neither was for sale. About the time of President Nelson's announcement, both were suddenly available. It was a miracle.[15]

The Lord has magnified our efforts in revising names that have long been attached to the Church.

Moving forward in faith, the name of the Mormon Tabernacle Choir was changed to The Tabernacle Choir at Temple Square. The website LDS.org, which received more than 21 million visits each month, was transitioned to ChurchofJesusChrist.org.[16] The name of LDS Business College was changed to Ensign College. The website Mormon.org was redirected into ChurchofJesusChrist.org. More than one thousand products that had the name "Mormon" or "LDS" attached to them have been renamed. Faithful Latter-day Saints have adjusted their websites, podcasts, and Twitter accounts.

We adopted a new symbol centered in Jesus Christ.

"At the center of the symbol is a representation of Thorvaldsen's marble statue the *Christus*. It portrays the resurrected, *living* Lord reaching out to embrace all who will come unto Him.

"Symbolically, Jesus Christ is standing under an arch [reminding] us of the resurrected Savior emerging from the tomb."[17]

The typography of The Church of Jesus Christ of Latter-day Saints has been adapted in more than 50 languages. New domain names have been acquired across the world.

Appreciation for the Help of Others

We appreciate the many good and gracious people who have honored our desire to be called by our correct name. I read an article recently that quoted a Catholic cardinal referring to "the Latter-day Saints."[18] As I visited with a leader of a Christian church a month ago in the eastern United States, he referred to the Church in his first reference with our entire name and followed it up more than once with "the Church of Jesus Christ."

We realized that adding six words to our name would not be ideal for the media, but, as President Nelson foretold, "responsible media will be sympathetic in responding to our request."[19] Thank you for extending to us the same consideration given cultural, athletic, political, or community organizations by using our preferred name.

There will be a few who, hoping to detract from or diminish the seriousness of our mission, will continue to call us "Mormons" or "the Mormon Church." With courtesy, we again ask the fair-minded of the media to honor our desire to be called by our name of nearly 200 years.

The Courage of the Latter-day Saints

There are thousands and thousands of Latter-day Saints who have courageously proclaimed the name of the Church. As we do our part, others will follow. I love this story from Tahiti.

Ten-year-old Iriura Jean resolved to follow the counsel of President Nelson.

"In her school class they discussed their weekend . . . and Iriura talked about . . . church.

"Her teacher, Vaite Pifao, said, 'Oh, so you are a Mormon?'

"Iriura stated boldly, 'No, . . . I am a member of The Church of Jesus Christ of Latter-day Saints!'

"Her teacher replied, 'Yes, . . . you are a Mormon.'

"Iriura insisted, 'No teacher, I am a member of The Church of Jesus Christ of Latter-day Saints!'

"Ms. Pifao was amazed at Iriura's conviction and wondered why she was so insistent on using [the] long name of her church. [She decided to learn more about the Church.]

"[Later, as Sister] Vaite Pifao was baptized [she expressed gratitude] that Iriura heeded the counsel of President Nelson."[20]

"The name of the Church is not negotiable." Let us go forward in faith. When we willingly follow the counsel of the Lord as revealed through His living prophet, especially if it runs counter to our initial thinking, requiring humility and sacrifice, the Lord blesses us with additional spiritual power and sends His angels to support us and stand by us.[21] We receive the Lord's affirmation and His approval.

I am an eyewitness to the power of heaven that rests upon our beloved prophet, President Russell M. Nelson. His most sincere desire is to please the Lord and bless our Heavenly Father's children.

From sacred, personal experience, I testify of the Lord's love for him. He is the prophet of God.

I witness that Jesus is the Christ, the Son of God. In the name of Jesus Christ, amen.

Notes

1. See 3 Nephi 27:7–9; Doctrine and Covenants 115:4.
2. Russell M. Nelson, in "The Name of the Church," Newsroom, Aug. 16, 2018, newsroom .ChurchofJesusChrist.org.
3. "President Nelson Discusses the Name of the Church," Newsroom, Aug. 21, 2018, newsroom .ChurchofJesusChrist.org.
4. Russell M. Nelson, "The Correct Name of the Church," *Ensign* or *Liahona*, Nov. 2018, 87.
5. Russell M. Nelson, "The Temple and Your Spiritual Foundation," *Liahona*, Nov. 2021, 116.
6. Doctrine and Covenants 64:32.
7. *Teachings of Presidents of the Church: Joseph Smith* (2007), 137.
8. 2 Nephi 27:26.
9. 1 Nephi 15:18.
10. Doctrine and Covenants 101:17.
11. Russell M. Nelson, "Becoming Exemplary Latter-day Saints," *Ensign* or *Liahona*, Nov. 2018, 114.
12. See Henry B. Eyring, "Thus Shall My Church Be Called," *Liahona*, Oct. 2021, 6–9.
13. Lauri Ahola, "Using the Full Name of the Church Was Awkward but Worth It" (digital-only article), *Liahona*, Apr. 2020, ChurchofJesusChrist.org.
14. Russell M. Nelson, "The Correct Name of the Church," 89.
15. The Church's Intellectual Property Office had been monitoring the domain name of ChurchofJesusChrist.org since 2006, and it had not been available. It was remarkable that it was offered for sale about the same time as President Nelson's announcement, and the Church purchased the domain name at a very modest amount.
    In the same manner, the Church had begun monitoring the status and availability of the domain name ChurchofJesusChrist.com since 2011. Surprisingly, it too became available in August 2018 and was also purchased.
16. In the October 2018 general conference, President Nelson said:
    "Brothers and sisters, there are many worldly arguments against restoring the correct name of the Church. Because of the digital world in which we live and with search engine optimization that helps all of us find information we need almost instantly—including information about the Lord's Church—critics say that a correction at this point is unwise. . . .
    ". . . I promise you that if we will do our best to restore the correct name of the Lord's Church, He whose Church this is will pour down His power and blessings upon the heads of the Latter-day Saints" ("The Correct Name of the Church," 88, 89).
    Since the transition of LDS.org to ChurchofJesusChrist.org, the domain authority (the ability and power of a site to rank in search engines) is stronger than it was previously. For example, the ChurchofJesusChrist.org home page is now, and has been for more than a year, the top search result in the United States on Google when someone searches for the term "church," where previously it could not claim this distinction.
17. Russell M. Nelson, "Opening the Heavens for Help," *Ensign* or *Liahona*, May 2020, 73.
18. See Tad Walch, "'If We Can't Get Along, It's Downright Sinful': The Partnership between Catholics and Latter-day Saints," *Deseret News*, July 1, 2021, deseret.com.
19. Russell M. Nelson, "The Correct Name of the Church," 89.
20. "The Correct Name of the Church: A Tahitian Story," Pacific Newsroom, Sept. 15, 2019, news-nz.ChurchofJesusChrist.org.
21. See Doctrine and Covenants 84:88.

MAKE TIME FOR THE LORD

PRESIDENT RUSSELL M. NELSON

President of The Church of Jesus Christ of Latter-day Saints

My dear brothers and sisters, for two days we have been well taught by servants of the Lord who have sought diligently to know what He would have them say.

We have been given our charge for the next six months. Now the question is, how will we be different because of what we have heard and felt?

The pandemic has demonstrated how quickly life can change, at times from circumstances beyond our control. However, there are many things we *can* control. We set our own priorities and determine how we use our energy, time, and means. We decide how we will treat each other. We choose those to whom we will turn for truth and guidance.

The voices and pressures of the world are engaging and numerous. But too many voices are deceptive, seductive, and can pull us off the covenant path. To avoid the inevitable heartbreak that follows, I plead with you today to counter the lure of the world by making time for the Lord in your life—each and every day.

If most of the information you get comes from social or other media, your ability to hear the whisperings of the Spirit will be diminished. If you are not also seeking the Lord through daily prayer and gospel study, you leave yourself vulnerable to philosophies that may be intriguing but are not true. Even Saints who are otherwise faithful can be derailed by the steady beat of Babylon's band.

My brothers and sisters, I plead with you to make time for the Lord! Make your own spiritual foundation firm and able to stand the test of time by doing those things that allow the Holy Ghost to be with you *always*.

Never underestimate the profound truth that "the Spirit speaketh . . . of things as they *really* are, and of things as they *really* will be."[1] "It will show unto you all things what ye should do."[2]

Nothing invites the Spirit more than fixing your focus on Jesus

197

Christ. Talk of Christ, rejoice in Christ, feast upon the words of Christ, and press forward with steadfastness in Christ.[3] Make your Sabbath a delight as you worship Him, partake of the sacrament, and keep His day holy.[4]

As I emphasized this morning, please make time for the Lord in His holy house. Nothing will strengthen your spiritual foundation like temple service and temple worship.

We thank all who are working on our new temples. They are being built all over the world. Today I am pleased to announce our plans to build more temples at or near the following locations: Kaohsiung, Taiwan; Tacloban, Philippines; Monrovia, Liberia; Kananga, Democratic Republic of the Congo; Antananarivo, Madagascar; Culiacán, Mexico; Vitória, Brazil; La Paz, Bolivia; Santiago West, Chile; Fort Worth, Texas; Cody, Wyoming; Rexburg North, Idaho; Heber Valley, Utah; and reconstruction of the Provo Utah Temple after the Orem Utah Temple is dedicated.

I love you, dear brothers and sisters. The Lord knows you and loves you. He is your Savior and your Redeemer. He leads and guides His Church. He will lead and guide *you* in your personal life if you will *make time for Him* in your life—each and every day.

May God be with you until we meet again, I pray in the sacred name of Jesus Christ, amen.

Notes

1. Jacob 4:13; emphasis added.
2. 2 Nephi 32:5.
3. See 2 Nephi 31:20.
4. See Exodus 31:13, 16; Isaiah 58:13.